MICHEL ROUX JR

COOKING WITH THE MASTER CHEF

WEIDENFELD & NICOLSON

MICHEL ROUX JR

COOKING WITH THE MASTER CHEF

Contents

This is my fifth book for Orion and it is compiled as a result of the extraordinary and unexpected response to my appearance as a judge on *MasterChef: The Professionals*. I have always resisted the siren call of television, except where I can see a way of helping fellow professionals or youngsters who need help starting off their careers. Two series with those qualities appealed to me, the amateur *MasterChef*, where I was able to help the winner, Dhruv Baker, with a placement at Le Gavroche, as well as the winner of professional *MasterChef*, Steve Groves. I am also involved in a new series called *Service,* in which I have been asked to help young men and women learn about front of house work of all kinds, with a view to getting them placements in anything from fast-food establishments to smart restaurants.

My appearance on *MasterChef* sparked an interest in my earlier books, many of which were out of print, so this is a compendium of my recipes; many of which have been simplified for the home cook.

My first book was the *Le Gavroche Cookbook*, based on my cooking at the restaurant which I took over from my father Albert, nearly 20 years ago. Le Gavroche has two Michelin stars and we aim to give our clientele as good a gastronomic experience as we can – so there is a sprinkling of fairly advanced recipes in this book for the more adventurous cook. I have turned down the notch as far as ingredients and techniques are concerned on a number of the more difficult ones.

The next was a book on matching food and wine, which is a particular passion of mine. From the age of 10 or so, like all good French children, I was introduced to watered down wine. Not too much later I was instructed to 'put your nose in that'; first to sniff the aroma, and then to taste the wine itself. I made the point that we are becoming more continental in our approach to food by the day – that food is not just about refuelling but is one of life's greatest pleasures – and that to enhance the pleasure it should very often be accompanied by a glass or two of wine. The recipes were chosen so that food and its accompanying wine would work well together; indeed, be much better than the sum of each part, and advice was given on difficult foods and those which react badly to wines.

My third book was *The Marathon Chef: Food for Getting Fit*, so called because I am an obsessive runner; running every day after the lunch service is finished and before returning for the evening stint. With sixteen marathons under my belt and some decent times, I felt I knew a bit – not only about getting fit (in terms of the type of diet required to maximize energy and stamina) but also what might taste delicious too. Interestingly, I found that running made me less tempted to eat heavy, fatty foods and I learned to tailor delicious food combinations, which not only worked for me in training, but have now worked their way on to the menu at Le Gavroche and have become firm favourites.

My most recent book was my life story to date, called *A Life in the Kitchen* and this had many recipes from the different eras of my life; from growing up in a household dominated by food, as an apprentice to famous chefs in France, doing my national service in the French army as a conscript in the kitchens of the Elysée Palace, working with my father and uncle in the Roux family business, cooking at home with my wife and daughter, and finally a chapter on Le Gavroche.

For me, my family was my first and lasting influence. They are imbued with that French reverence for food – everything related to food is taken seriously. The ingredients must be the best, they must be in season, and due consideration is given to how to cook them to the best advantage. Meals are always taken sitting down and never hurried. I inherited from my mother and father and my uncle Michel a great love of food and of cooking. The recipes in this book are taken from many years of cooking for others and for my family. Bon appetit!

Breads

Rich Brioche

15g fresh yeast
500g plain flour, sifted
6 eggs
2 teaspoons salt

50g sugar
300g butter, room temperature
1 egg, beaten, for glaze

Makes 1 large loaf

Put the yeast, along with a few drops of water to soften it, into the bowl of an electric mixer fitted with a dough hook. Add the flour, the eggs one at a time, and the salt and sugar to the yeast and slowly knead together. You can do this by hand, but it's actually better when kneaded by machine.

After 5 minutes the dough should be smooth and elastic. Add the butter and continue to knead at a slightly faster speed for 10 minutes. Make sure all the butter is well incorporated. Put the dough in a large clean bowl, cover with clingfilm and chill in the refrigerator for 12 hours. After 4 hours, knock the dough down by punching it firmly to release the fermentation gases.

Preheat the oven to 200°C/Gas 6. When ready to cook the brioche, tip the dough out on to a floured surface and shape into balls or roll into loaf tins. Leave in a warm, draught-free place until risen by a third, then brush with the beaten egg. Bake in the oven until golden. A loaf will need about 40 minutes and individual brioche about 15 minutes.

Wholemeal Bread

Leavening
15g fresh yeast
250ml warm water
100g strong white flour, sifted
150g wholemeal flour, sifted

Final mix
3 teaspoons salt
250ml warm water
300g spelt flour, sifted
300g rye flour, sifted

Makes 2 loaves

Bread is not difficult to make once you get the hang of it, and home-made loaves are worth the effort. The loaves can be made in an electric mixer with a dough hook or if you would like to make the bread by hand, knead for 10 minutes or so. I use fresh yeast but you can use dried if you prefer.

This bread is made in two stages. First, the leavening: dissolve the yeast in the water, then mix with the flours. Cover and leave to rise in a warm, draught-free place for about 1 hour or until it has doubled in volume.

Put the leavening mixture into the bowl of an electric mixer fitted with a dough hook. To make the final mix, dissolve the salt in the water, and add to the leavening with the flours. Beat at low speed until homogenous. Cover and leave to rise again for about 2 hours or until doubled in volume.

Knock the dough back, place on a floured surface, preferably marble or wood, and shape into large round loaves (550g) or individual rolls (40g). Put the loaves or rolls on a baking tray, cover and leave to rise for about 1 hour.

Preheat the oven to 230°C/Gas 8 and put a small container of water into the oven to create steam and stop the bread drying out.

Using a razor blade or very sharp knife, score the tops to about 6mm deep and immediately place in the oven. Bake the loaves for about 1 hour and the rolls for about 20 minutes or until the bread sounds hollow when tapped on the bottom.

Olive Oil Bread

12g fresh yeast
275ml warm water
500g strong, unbleached
  stoneground bread flour, sifted

4 tablespoons olive oil
1 heaped teaspoon fine salt
milk, for brushing
a pinch of coarse sea salt

Makes 1 loaf

Dissolve the yeast in the water, then add the flour. Knead in an electric mixer fitted with a dough hook for 15 minutes until silken and elastic. Add the olive oil and fine salt and knead again for 5 minutes. Cover and leave to rise in a warm, draught-free place for 40 minutes or until doubled in volume.

Knock the dough back and form it into a long loaf. Place on a non-stick baking sheet, cover and leave to rise again for 20 minutes.

Preheat the oven to 230°C/Gas 8 and put a small container of water into the oven to create steam and stop the bread drying out.

Lightly brush the top of the loaf with milk, add a sprinkling of coarse sea salt, then bake in the oven for 30 minutes or until the bread sounds hollow when tapped on the bottom. Leave to cool on a wire rack.

Soft Rye Bread Buns

30g milk powder
40g fresh yeast
600ml lukewarm water
600g strong white flour, sifted
400g dark rye flour, sifted

30g fine salt
1 tablespoon caster sugar
100g unsalted butter, melted

Makes 12–15 buns

Dissolve the milk powder and yeast in the water, then add the sifted flours.

Gently knead in an electric mixer fitted with a dough hook for 1 minute. Add the salt and sugar, increase the speed a little and knead for a further 5 minutes until smooth. After 3 minutes, bring down the dough from the top of the hook so that it mixes well with the rest, then pour in the lukewarm melted butter and knead until completely amalgamated. Cover the dough with a wet cloth and leave to rise in a warm, draught-free place for 30 minutes or until it has doubled in volume.

Once it has risen, knock back the dough, place it on a floured surface and shape into buns weighing 120g each. Place the buns on a baking tray, dust with flour, cover and leave to rise again for 20 minutes or until nearly doubled in size.

Preheat the oven to 230°C/Gas 8 and put a small container of water into the oven to create steam and stop the buns drying out.

Bake in the oven for about 16 minutes, then leave to cool on a wire rack.

Herb and Celery Soda Bread

250g wholemeal flour, sifted
250g strong, unbleached bread
  flour, sifted
1 teaspoon bicarbonate of soda
1 teaspoon celery salt
1 teaspoon salt
1 medium onion, diced
2 celery sticks, diced

65g butter
2 teaspoons celery seeds
250ml milk
juice of 1 lemon
1 bunch of mint, chopped
2 bunches of parsley, chopped
1 bunch of lovage (or celery
  leaf), chopped

Makes one loaf

Preheat the oven to 200°C/Gas 6 and put a small container of water into the oven to create steam and stop the bread drying out.

Mix the wholemeal and unbleached bread flours, bicarbonate of soda and salts together.

Sweat the onion and celery in a pan along with half of the butter and the celery seeds until soft, but not coloured. Take the pan off the heat and leave to cool.

Rub the rest of the butter into the flour and add the cooled onion and celery, with all their pan juices, and mix well. Make a well in the centre and pour in the milk and lemon juice. Mix the flour into the liquid to make a soft but not too sticky dough and add the chopped herbs. Turn the dough on to a floured surface and knead well, shaping it into an oblong loaf.

Put the dough into a lightly greased 900g loaf tin, and using a sharp knife, cut a deep cross into the dough.

Bake in the oven for 40–50 minutes or until the bread sounds hollow when tapped on the bottom. Leave to cool on a wire rack.

Irish Soda Bread

250g wholemeal flour, sifted
50g strong white flour, sifted
50g oatmeal
50g wheatgerm
1½ teaspoons bicarbonate
  of soda

1½ teaspoons salt
1 tablespoon light
  muscovado sugar
1 large egg
300ml buttermilk

Makes 1 loaf

Preheat the oven to 190°C/Gas 5 and put a small container of water into the oven to create steam and stop the bread drying out.

Mix the dry ingredients together and make a well in the centre. Break the egg into the well. Using your fingertips, gradually work in some of the flour and pour in the buttermilk until all has been absorbed. The dough should be soft but not too sticky – add a little flour if it is – and don't overwork it.

Make the dough into a loaf shape, place on a baking tray and bake in the oven for 1 hour. Leave to cool on a wire rack.

Rich Grain and Malt Bread

20g fresh yeast
450ml warm water
200g strong unbleached bread
  flour, sifted
200g spelt flour, sifted
100g wholemeal flour, sifted
100g rye flour, sifted

1 level tablespoon salt
3 tablespoons liquid extract of malt
1 tablespoon each of
  millet, rolled oats,
  linseed, sunflower seeds,
  bran, wheatgerm

Makes 2 loaves

Dissolve the yeast in half the warm water, then add the flours, salt, malt and whatever seeds and grains you are using. Knead by hand or in an electric mixer fitted with a dough hook, gradually adding more warm water.

When the dough is elastic, but not sticky, stop adding water. Continue to knead for another 10 minutes. In general, the more water in the dough the lighter the bread, but this bread is better if fairly heavy. Cover and leave to rise in a warm, draught-free place for 90 minutes.

Knock the dough back, turn it onto a floured surface and divide in half. Put the loaves into non-stick 450g loaf tins, cover and leave to rise again for 40 minutes.

Preheat the oven to 230°C/Gas 8 and put a small container of water into the oven to create steam and stop the bread drying out.

Bake in the oven for 10 minutes, then turn the oven down to 200°C/Gas 6 and bake for a further 30 minutes or until the bread sounds hollow when tapped on the bottom. Leave to cool on a wire rack.

Ceps and Confit Garlic Bread

60g dried ceps, sliced
425ml warm water
25g fresh yeast
400g strong white flour, sifted
1 tablespoon olive oil
100g spelt flour, sifted
100g rye flour, sifted

1 level tablespoon salt
1 tablespoon thyme leaves

Garlic Confit
12 garlic cloves
coarse sea salt
2 tablespoons olive oil

Makes 1 large loaf

Cover the ceps with 150ml of the warm water and leave to soak for 30 minutes.

Dissolve the yeast in the remaining water, then stir in the white flour using a wooden spatula. Cover and leave to rise in a warm, draught-free place until doubled in volume.

Drain the ceps, reserving the soaking water and pan-fry them in the olive oil for about 1 minute. Drain again and set aside.

Put the soaking water, the remaining flours, salt, thyme and the risen dough in an electric mixer fitted with a dough hook and knead on low speed for 10 minutes. Scrape down the edges and the hook and knead for a further 2 minutes. Cover and leave to rise again for 30 minutes. Knock back the dough, then gently work in the ceps and garlic without breaking them up. Do this by folding the bread over on itself several times. Shape the dough into a loaf and place on a floured baking tray. Cover and leave to rise again for 30 minutes.

Preheat the oven to 220°C/Gas 7 and put a small container of water into the oven to create steam and stop the bread drying out. Bake in the oven for 35–40 minutes.

Garlic confit

Preheat the oven to 170°C/Gas 3. Peel the garlic cloves, blanch in boiling water and drain. Put them on a piece of foil, then sprinkle with a little sea salt and a generous amount of olive oil. Wrap the garlic up loosely by bringing the corners of the foil together to make a 'bag'. Put into an ovenproof dish and bake in the oven for 1 hour, shaking the bag 3–4 times. Leave to cool before using.

Italian Ciabatta

12g fresh yeast
200ml warm water
265g strong white flour, sifted
1 teaspoon salt
3 tablespoons olive oil

Makes 1 loaf

Dissolve the yeast in the warm water, then add the flour and salt. The mixture will feel wet and sticky at first but don't add any more flour. Knead the dough for about 5–6 minutes until smooth.

Lightly oil a bowl with a little of the olive oil and put in the dough. Cover with clingfilm and leave in a warm, draught-free place for 40 minutes.

Knock back the dough and add the rest of the olive oil, but don't overwork it. Put the dough on a floured baking tray and shape into a loaf, about 28cm long. Flatten it lightly and flour the top. Cover with a dry cloth and leave to rise again for 40 minutes.

Preheat the oven to 220°C/Gas 7 and put a small container of water into the oven to create steam and stop the bread drying out.

Bake in the oven for 30–35 minutes. Leave to cool on a wire rack.

Fougasse Bread with Olives

20g fresh yeast
300ml lukewarm water
500g strong unbleached bread flour, sifted
1 heaped teaspoon salt
85g mixed pitted olives, best quality, not the ones in brine
4 tablespoons olive oil
1 tablespoon thyme and rosemary leaves

Makes 1 large loaf

Dissolve the yeast in the lukewarm water, then add the flour and salt and mix together to make a dough. Knead in an electric mixer fitted with a dough hook or by hand for at least 12 minutes. Then cover and leave to rise in a warm, draught-free place for 45 minutes.

Turn the dough out on to a floured surface and mix in the olives, olive oil and thyme and rosemary leaves. Make the dough into a ball, then roll it out to 15mm thick. Transfer the dough to a non-stick baking tray, then cut through it six times to make a leaf pattern, pulling on the dough to make the holes bigger. Cover and leave to rise again for 20–30 minutes.

Preheat the oven to 230°C/Gas 8 and put a small container of water into the oven to create steam and stop the bread drying out.

Bake in the oven for about 35–40 minutes or until the bread sounds hollow when tapped on the bottom. Leave to cool on a wire rack.

Goat's Cheese Bread

15g fresh yeast
250ml warm water
600g spelt flour or unbleached
  white bread flour, sifted
60g boiled potato, crushed
1 heaped teaspoon fine salt

65g dry goat's cheese (crottin
  or similar)
1 tablespoon thyme and
  rosemary leaves
coarse sea salt
2 tablespoons olive oil

Makes 12 rolls

Dissolve the yeast in the warm water, then add the flour, crushed potato and fine salt. Knead in an electric mixer fitted with a dough hook or by hand for 10 minutes until elastic and smooth. Cover and leave to rise in a warm, draught-free place for about 45 minutes or until it has doubled in volume.

Knock the dough back and divide into 12 rolls or roll out to make 1 large loaf about 2cm thick. Place on a lightly oiled baking sheet. Crumble the cheese and push it on to the surface of the bread. Sprinkle with thyme, rosemary and a little coarse sea salt, drizzle with the olive oil and leave to rise again for 15 minutes.

Preheat the oven to 220°C/Gas 7 and put a small container of water into the oven to create steam and stop the bread drying out.

Bake the rolls in the oven for 20 minutes or the loaf for 30–40 minutes until the bread sounds hollow when tapped on the bottom. Leave to cool on a wire rack.

Black Pepper Baps

20g fresh yeast
300ml warm milk
500g strong white flour, sifted
1 tablespoon caster sugar

2 teaspoons salt
20g cracked black peppercorns

Makes 12–14 baps

Dissolve the yeast in the milk, then gradually add the flour, sugar, salt and peppercorns. Knead the dough in an electric mixer fitted with a dough hook or by hand until it is elastic yet supple. Cover and leave to rise in a warm, draught-free place for about 30 minutes or until it has doubled in volume.

Knock the dough back and place on a floured surface. Divide it into 12–14 baps weighing about 60g, cup your hand over each bap and 'turn' them until smooth and perfectly round. Put these on a floured baking tray, cover and leave to rise again for 20 minutes.

Preheat the oven to 220°C/Gas 7 and put a small container of water into the oven to create steam and stop the rolls drying out.

Bake in the oven for 15–20 minutes. Leave to cool on a wire rack.

Focaccia with Basil, Garlic and Anchovies

25g fresh yeast
350ml lukewarm water
750g strong white flour, sifted
3 tablespoons olive oil
1 heaped teaspoon sugar
2 teaspoons salt

12 anchovy fillets
1 bunch of basil, leaves only
2 garlic cloves, coarsely
  chopped
crushed black pepper

Makes 1 large loaf

Dissolve the yeast in the lukewarm water, then add to the flour and knead in the olive oil, sugar and salt until smooth and elastic. Cover and leave to rise in a warm, draught-free place for 30–40 minutes or until it has doubled in volume.

Roll the dough out on a lightly floured surface to a thickness of 2cm. Place on a non-stick baking sheet, make several slashes in the centre of the bread and pull the dough gently from the edges. Cover the surface evenly with anchovies, basil leaves and coarsely chopped garlic. Sprinkle with a little crushed black pepper and leave to rise again for 20 minutes.

Preheat the oven to 220°C/Gas 7 and put a small container of water into the oven to create steam and stop the bread drying out.

Bake in the oven for 20–30 minutes or until the bread sounds hollow when tapped on the bottom. Leave to cool on a wire rack.

Fruit and Nut Bread

50g fresh yeast
1.25 litres warm water
1.2kg strong white flour, sifted
35g salt
125g light rye flour

375g wholemeal flour
60g dried apricots, sliced
100g sultanas
100g walnuts
60g hazelnuts

Makes 3 loaves

Mix the yeast in a litre of the warm water, then add the white flour and salt. Knead the dough in an electric mixer fitted with a dough hook or by hand for about 10 minutes or until it is elastic and comes away from the sides of the bowl. Cover with a damp cloth and leave to rise in a warm, draught-free place for about 60–90 minutes or until it has doubled in volume.

Knead again, by machine or hand, and add the remaining 250ml warm water with the rye and wholemeal flours. Continue kneading until the flours are completely amalgamated, then gently mix in the fruit and nuts by hand.

Shape into 3 long loaves and place on a non-stick baking sheet or put into lightly oiled bread tins. Cover the loaves with a damp cloth and leave to rise again by a third, which should take about 30 minutes.

Preheat the oven to 250°C/Gas 9 and put a small container of water into the oven to create steam and stop the bread drying out.

Put the loaves into the hot oven and turn down the temperature to 220°C/Gas 7. Bake for about 30–35 minutes or until the bread sounds hollow when tapped on the bottom. Leave to cool on a wire rack. Great toasted for breakfast or with cheese.

Corn and Fennel Seed Bread

30g fresh yeast
150ml warm water
2 tablespoons honey
200g strong white flour, sifted
250ml milk

250g fine polenta
1 teaspoon salt
2 tablespoons fennel seeds
1 tablespoon milk, for brushing

Makes 1 large loaf

Dissolve the yeast in the warm water and honey, then add half the flour to make a very wet paste. Cover and leave to rise in a warm, draught-free place for 30 minutes.

Put the rest of the ingredients into the bowl of an electric mixer fitted with a dough hook – keep back 1 tablespoon of fennel seeds to garnish the loaf. Pour in the first mix and work to a smooth, elastic dough.

Put the dough in a large lightly oiled 24cm x 8cm loaf tin or divide it into mini-loaf tins, about 3cm x 5cm. Cover and leave to rise again for 30 minutes.

Preheat the oven to 220°C/Gas 7 and put a small container of water into the oven to create steam and stop the bread drying out.

Brush the top of the bread with a little milk and sprinkle with the remaining seeds. Bake in the oven for 20–30 minutes depending on size. Leave to cool on a wire rack.

Cheese and Marjoram Rolls

25g fresh yeast
460ml warm water
100ml warm milk, plus extra
  for brushing
1kg strong, unbleached,
  stoneground bread flour, sifted
2 teaspoons salt
20g caster sugar

1 egg
2 tablespoons olive oil
100g Parmesan cheese,
  freshly grated
1 bunch of marjoram,
  leaves only
300g Cheddar or Emmental
  cheese, cut into 30 thin slices

Makes 30 rolls

Dissolve the yeast in the warm water and milk, then add the flour, salt, sugar, egg and olive oil. Knead by hand or in an electric mixer fitted with a dough hook for 12–15 minutes. Cover and leave to rise in a warm, draught-free place for 90 minutes.

Knock back the dough and incorporate the Parmesan cheese and marjoram without overworking. Divide the dough into 30 pieces, weighing about 60g, and place on a non-stick baking tray. Cover and leave to rise again for 20 minutes.

Preheat the oven to 190°C/Gas 5 and put a small container of water into the oven to create steam and stop the bread drying out.

Brush the rolls with a little milk. Using a sharp pair of scissors, cut a deep cross on the top of each roll and insert a thin slice of Cheddar or Emmental. Bake in the oven for 25–30 minutes. Leave to cool on a wire rack.

Bacon Cornbread

150g smoked bacon
vegetable oil, for cooking
100g plain flour
2 teaspoons baking powder
1 teaspoon salt

250g polenta (yellow cornmeal)
1 egg, beaten
375ml buttermilk
3 tablespoons maple syrup

Makes about 60 canapés

These bacon cornbread canapés can be served plain or with a little cream cheese piped on top. Cornbread can also be made in Yorkshire pudding pans and served as an accompaniment to soups or stews.

Preheat the oven to 190°C/Gas 5. Blanch the bacon in boiling water for 1 minute, then cut into very small lardons. Fry the lardons in a non-stick pan with a tiny drop of oil until slightly crisp. Take the pan off the heat and leave to cool with the bacon fat still in the pan.

Sift the flour, baking powder and salt into a bowl, add the polenta, egg and buttermilk and beat with a wooden spoon until smooth. Fold in the maple syrup and bacon, including its fat.

Pour this mixture into well-buttered small cake tins, about 3cm in diameter, and cook in the oven for 10–15 minutes or until firm to the touch and a knife pulls out clean when inserted into the centre. These should be eaten on the day they are made.

Chelsea Buns

500g strong bread flour
75g caster sugar
1 teaspoon salt
75g butter
35g yeast
250ml tepid milk

1 egg
50g butter, melted
50g sultanas
grated zest of ½ lemon
½ tablespoon cinnamon
½ tablespoon icing sugar

Makes 15 buns

We all love baking in our family. These little buns are gloriously delicious and can be eaten either straight from the oven, or left to cool then lightly toasted with a slab of Brittany salted butter.

Sift the flour, sugar and salt together, then gently rub in the butter. Dissolve the yeast in the tepid milk and add the egg. Gradually mix this with the flour until you have a dough texture and dust the work surface with extra flour to avoid it sticking. Place the dough in a bowl, cover and leave to rise in a warm, draught-free place until it has doubled in volume.

Knock the dough back and roll out into a rectangle measuring about 20cm x 40cm. Brush with the melted butter and sprinkle with the sultanas and lemon zest. Mix together the cinnamon and icing sugar and sprinkle over the dough. Roll up the dough, starting from the longest edge, and cut the roll into about 15 pieces. Put the buns on a non-stick baking tray, making sure they are not too close together, and leave to rise again for 15–20 minutes.

Preheat the oven to 220°C/Gas 7. Bake the buns in the oven for 15 minutes. The buns should be golden brown, yet moist, and all stuck together. Leave to cool a little on a wire rack before separating.

Croissants

45g fresh yeast
400ml warm water
40g milk powder
800g flour, sifted
80g sugar

20g salt
40g butter, melted
300g butter, room temperature
1 egg, beaten

Makes 30 small croissants

Dissolve the yeast in the warm water and milk powder. Add to the flour, sugar, salt and the melted butter. Knead well in an electric mixer fitted with a dough hook or by hand for about 4–5 minutes until smooth and everything is incorporated, but do not overwork. Cover and leave to rise in a warm, draught-free place until it has doubled in volume.

Roll the dough out to 21cm x 29cm (A4 size). Place the softened butter in the middle and fold over all the edges of the dough to envelope it completely. Dust with flour and gently roll out to a rectangle about 40cm x 26cm. Take both ends, fold them to the centre and fold again to make a much smaller rectangle. Wrap in clingfilm and chill in the refrigerator for an hour. Repeat the process of rolling out and folding the dough.

Roll out the dough on a floured surface to a thickness of 1cm and cut triangles with a base of 12cm. Roll these triangles towards the point, then bring the points together to form the croissant shape. Place the croissants on a baking tray and leave to rise again for about 20 minutes.

Preheat the oven to 180°C/Gas 4. Brush the croissants with beaten egg and bake in the oven until cooked. The croissants can be frozen, once rolled, and taken out of the freezer an hour before cooking.

Soups, Pâtés and Terrines

Squash and Shrimp Soup with Nutmeg

4 x 175g squash or 1 x 700g
pumpkin (unpeeled weight)
4 shallots, diced
olive oil

salt and pepper
grated nutmeg
1 litre chicken stock (page 208)
200g peeled brown shrimps

Serves 4

If using small squash, such as acorn squash, the soup can be served to your guests in the hollowed-out skins. If you are using a big pumpkin, then it can be brought to the table as a tureen.

If using the squash or pumpkin for serving this soup, slice off the top and hollow out the flesh and seeds using a spoon. Otherwise, cut away the skin with a knife. Cut the flesh into very small dice.

Sweat the squash or pumpkin and shallots in a little olive oil until soft but not coloured. Season with a generous amount of salt, pepper and nutmeg, then pour in the stock. Bring to a simmer and cook for 20 minutes.

Take the pan off the heat and, using a hand-held blender or food processor, blend until smooth. Add the shrimps just before serving.

Duck and Vermicelli Soup Flavoured with Lemongrass

4 turnips
4 courgettes
1 small leek
2 large duck legs, about 400g
salt and pepper
1 tablespoon demerara sugar
8 star anise
2 celery sticks
1 onion, cut into quarters

about 2 litres water
1 lemongrass
1 lime
160g Chinese rice vermicelli,
  cooked
4 spring onions, thinly sliced
sesame oil, for drizzling
1 bunch coriander,
  leaves only

Serves 8

My daughter's favourite soup, and more often a meal. The duck legs can be substituted with good-quality chicken legs. A few drops of Tabasco works well for those that like a kick.

Cut the turnips into fine julienne strips, saving the trimmings for later. Cut the courgettes into juliennes, avoiding the core that may be a little soft. Prepare the leek in the same way, also keeping the trimmings. Blanch the vegetable juliennes briefly and refresh in iced water. The vegetables should still be crunchy. Drain and set aside.

Put the duck legs, salt, pepper, sugar, star anise, celery and onion into a large pot. Add the turnip and leek trimmings and cover with the water. Bring to a gentle simmer and skim well. Cut the outer stalk and top off the lemongrass and add to the pot, together with a little piece of lime peel from the lime. Simmer for 1 hour, then leave to cool for 30 minutes.

Once cool, remove the duck and shred, discarding the skin and bones. Pass the liquid through a fine sieve into a clean pan and check the seasoning. Bring to the boil, then add the precooked vermicelli, duck meat, vegetables, spring onions. Stir and cook until heated through.

Finish with a drizzle of sesame oil, coriander leaves and lime juice.

Chilled Mushroom Soup with Tapenade

200g mixed fresh mushrooms
50g butter
juice of 1 lemon
500ml chicken stock (page 208)
125ml double cream

1 tablespoon tapenade
salt and pepper
cayenne pepper, to taste
basil and chervil, chopped

Serves 4

Clean the mushrooms and cut into chunks, then cook in the butter over a low heat for 5 minutes. Add the lemon juice and stock, turn up the heat and boil for a further 5 minutes.

Purée in a blender until completely smooth. Pour into a bowl, cover and chill in the refrigerator for at least 1 hour.

Whip the cream until it forms soft peaks, then fold in the tapenade. Fold this mixture into the chilled mushroom soup, and season to taste with salt, pepper and cayenne pepper. Sprinkle with the chopped herbs just before serving.

Chestnut and Apple Soup with Rosemary

1kg fresh chestnuts
1 litre water
salt and pepper
2 tablespoons maple syrup

2 sprigs rosemary
4 apples, Coxes or similar,
  peeled, cored and finely diced

Serves 6

I was once ushered away at gunpoint from an area in the Cévennes region of France where the sweetest chestnuts are grown and gathered. The early season crop is highly prized and the locals protect their trees with vigour!

Preheat the oven to 230°C/Gas 8. Score the chestnuts with a sharp-pointed knife to prevent them exploding in the oven while roasting. Lay them out on a roasting tray and cook in the oven for 12–15 minutes. Leave to cool, then when cool enough to handle, remove the outer shells and the skin.

Keep 12 perfectly shaped chestnuts for the garnish and put the rest in a pan with the water. Bring to the boil, season, then add the maple syrup and rosemary and simmer for 20 minutes.

Take the pan off the heat, discard the rosemary and blend the soup until smooth. Return to the clean pan and add the apple. Cook for 3 minutes or until heated through before pouring into warm bowls and garnishing with the whole peeled chestnuts.

Lettuce Soup

100g dark outer lettuce leaves
1 tablespoon butter
300g potatoes, peeled and diced
200g ripe tomatoes, quartered

1.4 litres boiling water
salt and pepper
crème fraîche

Serves 4

My grandmother Germaine used to make this classic French soup. The original recipe calls for new season, tender round lettuce. However, being a good housekeeper with monetary constraints, she used any kind of lettuce, and only the outer dark-green leaves that were not as palatable as the sweet hearts in a salad.

Tear the lettuce leaves into pieces if large, then sweat in the butter. Add the diced potato and quartered tomatoes. Continue to cook for a further 5 minutes, then add the water. Simmer for 20 minutes or until the potatoes are cooked.

Season to taste, then blend until smooth or pass though a fine sieve if preferred. Delicious hot or cold, with or without a good spoonful of crème fraîche. Add a garnish of lettuce hearts and a little chopped tomato if you like.

Cock-a-leekie Soup

1.5 litres chicken stock
  (page 206)
salt and pepper
200g leeks

100g cooked chicken
100g prunes, stoned
chopped parsley

Serves 6

This soup is a good way to use up any leftover roast chicken. Use the carcass for making the stock. Only the yellow and white leaves of the leeks are used, so keep the rest of the leek for another recipe. Make sure the soup is served piping hot.

Put the stock in a large pan and bring to the boil. Season with salt and pepper.

Shred the yellow and white leaves of the leeks, then add them to the stock and leave to simmer for 15–20 minutes.

Cut the chicken and prunes into fine strips and add to the soup. Simmer for another 2 minutes, before checking the seasoning.

Sprinkle with chopped parsley and serve piping hot.

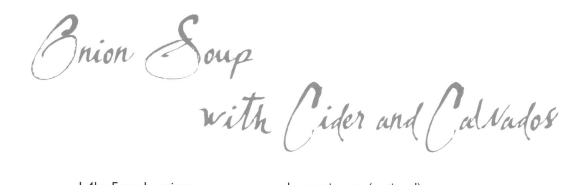

Onion Soup with Cider and Calvados

1.4kg French onions
1 tablespoon vegetable oil
45g butter
30g plain flour
750ml dry cider
1 bouquet garni
2.5 litres beef stock (page 207)
salt and pepper

sherry vinegar (optional)
6 egg yolks
3 tablespoons crème fraîche
6 tablespoons Calvados
1 country-style baguette,
 toasted
120g Gruyère, grated

Serves 6

It is most important that the onions are of top quality, firm and strong in taste. My favourites are a pink-fleshed French variety from Roscoff. You will need heatproof porcelain or earthenware dishes for this, as it is finished under the grill.

Cut the onions in half, slice thinly and place in a large, heavy-based saucepan with the oil and one-third of the butter. Cook over a high heat, stirring occasionally, until the onions start to caramelise. Turn the heat down and continue cooking until the onions are soft but still in slices, for about 20–30 minutes.

Meanwhile, make a brown roux by melting the remaining butter in a large, heavy-based pan. Add the flour and stir well over a medium heat, until light brown and nutty smelling. Pour two-thirds of the cider into the pan, whisking vigorously. Add the bouquet garni and bring to the boil. Add the stock and simmer for 30 minutes.

When the onions are soft, pour in the remaining cider and bring to the boil. Strain the thickened stock over the onions, stir and season well. Simmer for 15 minutes.

Preheat the grill. To serve, add a few drops of sherry vinegar to the soup. In each dish, lightly beat an egg yolk with ½ tablespoon of crème fraîche and 1 tablespoon of Calvados. Pour the soup on to this mixture, stirring. Place two or three slices of toasted baguette on the soup and top with a generous handful of cheese. Grill until the cheese begins to bubble, then serve immediately.

Rabbit Rillettes

1.2kg pork back fat
2 litres water
bouquet garni made from celery
　stick, small piece of leek, 2 bay
　leaves, 5–6 parsley stalks and
　thyme tied together with string
1 onion, studded with 2 cloves
1 carrot
3 garlic cloves, peeled

150g smoked bacon, diced
½ bottle dry white wine
salt and pepper
grated nutmeg
1.2kg rabbit, boned and cut up
400g pork shoulder, cut into
　dice
200ml dry white wine

Serves 15–20

This classic pâté can be kept for up to a month in a sterilized jar in the refrigerator, but why wait?

Cut the pork back fat into small cubes and put into a large saucepan. Cover with water, about 2 litres, and simmer for about 1 hour or until the fat has softened and become translucent and the water has evaporated.

Add the bouquet garni, onion, carrot, peeled garlic, smoked bacon and the half bottle of wine. Season generously with salt, pepper and nutmeg, remembering that when cold it will taste bland if it's not slightly over-seasoned now.

Add the rabbit and diced pork to the simmering mixture in the pan and stir well. Cover with a parchment paper and turn down the heat so the pan barely simmers. Cook, stirring occasionally, for about 2 hours until the meat is so soft it crumbles.

Take the pan off the heat and pour into a clean bowl set on ice. Add the 200ml wine and stir vigorously with a spatula until cold. The rillettes will change colour and turn opaque white from the emulsified fat. Put the rillettes into jars or a terrine and store in the refrigerator. Serve with hot toast and cornichons.

Chicken Liver Parfait

100ml port
100ml Madeira
50ml brandy
200g chicken livers
  (cleaned weight)
200g raw foie gras
3 shallots, chopped

400g butter
5 eggs
1 sprig thyme
1 garlic clove
salt and pepper
grated nutmeg

Serves 10–12

Once upon a time, this was on every menu in the country. It is now out of fashion but due a comeback. The foie gras is needed to give it richness. Liver is nearly always served with something sweet to eat and this also applies to drinks, so try old sweetened Oloroso sherry.

Preheat the oven to 140°C/Gas 1 and butter a 2cm x 8cm terrine. Pour the port, Madeira and brandy into a pan and reduce until syrupy.

Trim the chicken livers, making sure there are no green bile areas, which can be bitter. Put the chicken livers and foie gras into a blender or food processor and blitz until smooth. Sweat the shallots in a little butter and leave them to cool. Melt the rest of the butter. Add the shallots with the reduced alcohol and melted (not hot) butter in a stream to the liver mixture.

Add the eggs, one by one, thyme and garlic and continue to blitz. Season well, then pass the mixture through a fine sieve into the buttered terrine. Place the terrine in a bain-marie or a roasting pan filled with water and bring the water to a gentle simmer. Cover and cook in the oven for 1½–2 hours or until set. Leave to cool, then chill in the refrigerator overnight.

To serve, remove the skin that will have formed and make into quenelles by dipping a tablespoon into hot water. Alternatively, turn the parfait out of the terrine by running a hot knife around the edge and dipping the dish into hot water for a few seconds, then slice. Serve with melba toast, salad and chutney.

Duck Foie Gras with Confit Turnips

6 medium firm turnips
1 tablespoon caster sugar
2 tablespoons duck or goose fat
salt and pepper
125ml Madeira

250ml chicken stock (page 208)
1 tablespoon sherry vinegar
1 lobe of duck foie gras,
  about 500g

Serves 6

This is a dish I first came across when I was working as a young apprentice at the great Alain Chapel restaurant in France. Serve with a velvety Pinot Noir wine or a sweet red Banyuls.

Cut the turnips into 5mm slices. Toss the slices in caster sugar and put in a wide pan with the duck fat. Cook the turnips gently, turning frequently, until they are golden all over. Season and add the Madeira. Boil until the liquid has almost completely evaporated, then add the stock and reduce until syrupy. The turnips should be tender but still holding together. Finally splash in the sherry vinegar.

Cut the duck foie gras into six slices and season with salt and pepper. Place in a scalding hot pan and sear well until caramelised on both sides and cooked. Check the liver is cooked by pressing with a finger – it should give slightly under the pressure. Serve with the confit turnips.

Rabbit Terrine cooked in Chablis with Grain Mustard

1 rabbit (domestic, not wild, about 1.5kg)
2 tablespoons olive oil
1 carrot, diced
1 onion, diced
100g smoked bacon, diced
400ml Chablis wine
½ calf's foot, split in two
2 bay leaves
1 sprig thyme
1 litre chicken stock (page 208)
salt and pepper
2 tablespoons grain mustard
generous amount of flat leaf parsley, tarragon, and chervil, roughly chopped

Serves 8

Preheat the oven to 120°C/Gas ½. Prepare the rabbit by removing the heart and lungs, but if you like the liver and kidneys leave them in to cook with the rabbit.

Heat the olive oil in a large casserole dish and seal the rabbit on all sides. Add the carrot, onion and bacon and cook over a medium heat until lightly coloured. Add the wine and boil for 1 minute, then add the calf's foot, bay leaves, thyme and stock and season with salt and pepper. Bring to the boil, cover with a lid, and cook in the oven for 1½ hours.

Take out of the oven and leave to cool. When hand hot, pick all the meat off the bones and shred between your fingers into a bowl.

Pass the cooking liquid through a colander into a pan. Return the carrot and onion to the meat. Boil the cooking liquid and skim thoroughly to remove as much fat and scum as possible; reduce by a third and pour on to the meat. Stir in the mustard and herbs and check for seasoning, then pour into a porcelain terrine. Chill in the refrigerator for at least 12 hours.

Serve with toasted sourdough bread, and a little salad of chives, chervil, tarragon, watercress, wild rocket and dandelion dressed in red wine vinegar and a rich olive oil.

Smoked Haddock and Potato Terrine

2 x 300–400g fillets undyed
  smoked haddock
milk, for covering fish
6 medium potatoes such as
  Maris Piper
4 tablespoons olive oil

2 tablespoons red wine vinegar
1 tablespoon coarse grain
  mustard
salt and pepper
2 red onions, finely chopped
500g baby spinach leaves

Serves 10–12

Double line a 24cm x 8cm x 7cm terrine with clingfilm, overlapping the edges by at least 8cm.

Place the haddock fillets in a pan or baking tray large enough for them to lie flat and cover with a mixture of half milk and half water. Set the pan over a high heat and as soon as the liquid trembles and is too hot to put your fingers into, stop the cooking. Take the pan off the heat and leave to cool. The haddock will be cooked, but moist and delicate in texture. Once the haddock is cool, remove the bones and skin, keeping the pieces of fish as large as you can.

Cook the potatoes in their skins in a pan of boiling salted water, then leave to cool. When they are cool enough to handle, skin and cut into slices 1cm thick.

Make a vinaigrette with the olive oil, vinegar, mustard, salt and pepper, and pour some over the potatoes while they are still warm.

Fill the terrine with layers of potatoes and fish. Start with the potatoes, squaring them off to make them fit snugly, followed by a layer of fish, generously sprinkled with onion. Repeat the layers until the terrine is full. Fold over the clingfilm and weight the terrine down, either by putting another terrine of the same size on top or a piece of wood and some weights. Chill in the refrigerator for at least 6 hours or overnight.

Serve with a salad made with the baby spinach leaves, dressed in the leftover vinaigrette. If you're feeling extravagant, add a spoonful of caviar to each serving.

Ham and Cauliflower Terrine

8 slices of Parma ham
300g cauliflower, cut into florets
1 tablespoon butter
200g cooked ham, diced

4 eggs
200ml double cream
salt and pepper
nutmeg, grated

Serves 10–12

Wonderful for a picnic, and even better with the addition of a few shavings of summer truffle.

Preheat the oven to 140°C/Gas 1. Double line a 28cm x 8cm terrine or cake tin with clingfilm, then line the tin with the Parma ham, making sure the slices overlap the edges of the terrine.

Cook the cauliflower florets in a pan of boiling salted water until tender, then drain and leave to cool.

Heat the butter in a frying pan and toss in the diced ham. Once the ham is lightly browned, drain and add to the cauliflower. Beat the eggs with the cream and season with salt, pepper and nutmeg. Add the ham and cauliflower to the terrine, then pour in the egg and cream mixture.

Fold over the overlapping ham and clingfilm, then place the terrine in a bain-marie and bake in the oven for 1 hour.

Leave to cool completely before taking the terrine out of the tin. If you do have a truffle, add some shavings just before serving.

Wild Boar Pâté Flavoured with Juniper Berries

200g smoked belly pork
200g wild boar meat from
  the leg
1 tablespoon brandy
salt and pepper
2 shallots, finely chopped
1 garlic clove, finely chopped
200ml strong red wine

2 sprigs thyme
1 bay leaf
800g wild boar meat taken from
  shoulder
300g pork fat
6 juniper berries, crushed
10–12 thin slices Parma ham

Serves 8–10

My brother in law, Gerard, is always bringing home wild boar from his hunting trips, and this is a great way to use it up. Well worth the effort.

Remove the rind from the smoked belly and cut into pieces 1cm x 3cm. Cut the leg pieces in the same way and add to the smoked belly. Douse with brandy, season, then cover and chill in the refrigerator.

Bring the shallots, garlic and red wine to the boil. Add the thyme and bay leaf and reduce until almost dry. Discard the herbs, then let the shallot mix cool. Set aside.

Roughly cut the remaining meat into large cubes. Season with 2 teaspoons of salt and 1 teaspoon of pepper, and add the juniper berries. Cover and chill overnight.

The next day, mince the smoked belly mixture and beat well. Add the shallot mix and the cubed meat with its juices. Preheat the oven to 200°C/Gas 6 and butter a 20cm x 30cm terrine. Line the terrine with the Parma ham, overlapping over the sides. Press the mixture into the terrine and place in a bain-marie. Place in the oven for 15 minutes, then turn the oven down to 160°C/Gas 2–3, cover with buttered foil and continue to cook for 40 minutes.

Leave to cool for 30 minutes, then place a weight, about 500g, on top and leave for 2 hours. Chill in the refrigerator overnight. Serve with country-style bread.

Salads

Salade Lyonnaise

400g dandelion leaves or frisée
   salad
180g smoked streaky bacon
4 tablespoons olive oil
1 tablespoon white wine vinegar

1 small baguette bread
2 garlic cloves, cut in half
4 free-range eggs
2 tablespoons red wine vinegar
salt and pepper

Serves 4

This classic salad should be made with dandelion leaves, but they can be a little bitter for some people. If you are lucky enough to have a garden with untreated areas in it, you can pick your own leaves. Alternatively, use frisée salad.

Preheat the oven to 170°C/Gas 3. Wash and dry the salad leaves and put into a bowl. Cut the bacon into strips or batons, then place them in a non-stick pan with a drop of olive oil and cook slowly over a medium heat.

Meanwhile, put a saucepan of water on to boil with a generous splash of white wine vinegar. Cut the baguette into 20 thin slices and bake in the oven until dry and crisp. Rub the slices with the cut garlic.

Crack the eggs and carefully drop them into the simmering, vinegared water to poach. The eggs should take about 4 minutes for the whites to be cooked, with the yolk still very runny. Pour the bacon and fat onto the salad, with the bread, red wine vinegar and remaining olive oil. Season lightly with salt but generously with pepper, toss and place the drained, hot eggs on top.

Tiger Prawn and Apple Salad

18 tiger prawns, shelled and
deveined
6 tablespoons vegetable oil, plus
extra for smearing on prawns
salt and pepper
2 garlic cloves, finely chopped
2 teaspoons clear honey

1 teaspoon Madras curry
powder
juice of 2 limes
juice of 1 lemon
2 Granny Smith apples
3 Little Gem lettuce
1 bunch chives

Serves 6

Vibrant colours, fresh zingy tastes and contrasting textures, a perfect balance.

Preheat the grill. Smear the prawns with a little vegetable oil, then season with salt and pepper and put under the grill to cook.

Make a dressing with the garlic, oil, honey and curry powder, then add the lime juice and half of the lemon juice.

Cut the apples into matchsticks and place in a bowl of cold water with the remaining lemon juice to keep white.

Cut the lettuce into manageable pieces and cut the chives into matchsticks. Toss all the ingredients in the dressing. Season well and serve with the prawns on top.

Spicy Crab and Glass Noodle Salad

160g rice glass noodles
4cm piece of fresh ginger
1 red onion, thinly sliced
1 red chilli, thinly sliced
1 garlic clove, finely chopped
1 tablespoon crunchy peanut
  butter
salt and pepper
2 tablespoons fish sauce

1 tablespoon light
  muscovado sugar
4 tablespoons blended
  sesame oil
juice of 4 limes
200g picked fresh crab
  claw meat
coriander leaves

Serves 4

This is an easy oriental style salad that works well with all seafood, my favourite is crab but shrimps or grilled tiger prawns are just as delicious.

Pour boiling water over the noodles to cook according to the instructions on the packet, usually 3 minutes, then drain.

Peel the ginger and cut into very thin julienne strips. Toss the ginger, onion and chilli with the noodles.

Make a vinaigrette with the garlic, peanut butter, salt, pepper, fish sauce, sugar, sesame oil and lime juice. Dress the salad with the vinaigrette, then sprinkle the crab claw meat on top and garnish with sprigs of coriander.

Tunisian Grilled Vegetable Salad

6 plum tomatoes
salt and pepper
juice of 2 lemons
a pinch of saffron strands
2 teaspoons cumin seeds
½ teaspoon harissa
2 garlic cloves, chopped

2 tablespoons olive oil
12 new season onions
3 green peppers
3 red peppers
1 large courgette
2 aubergines
coriander leaves

Serves 6

Blanch the tomatoes in boiling water, refresh in iced water and skin. Cut them in half and chop roughly. Cook the tomato flesh in a scalding hot, non-stick pan for 2 minutes until it becomes pulpy. Add the seasoning, lemon juice, saffron, cumin seeds, harissa and chopped garlic, then take off the heat and whisk in the olive oil.

Preheat the grill. Cut the onions in half and grill on a cast-iron griddle, leaving them slightly crunchy. Roast the peppers under the hot grill until blackened all over, cover with clingfilm and leave to cool. When cool, peel off the black skin, remove the stalk, core and seeds, and cut into wide strips. Set aside.

Cut the courgette and aubergines into 6mm slices and grill on both sides. Leave to cool. Season the cold vegetables and arrange on plates with a little of the tomato dressing in between. Garnish with coriander leaves.

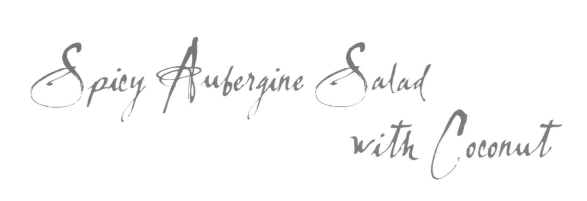

Spicy Aubergine Salad with Coconut

4 large aubergines
vegetable oil, for frying
salt
chilli powder
2 tablespoons tomato ketchup

1 tablespoon wholegrain
  Dijon mustard
juice of 1 lemon
2 spring onions, thinly sliced
50g coconut chips, toasted

Serves 6

This dish is adapted from a Sri Lankan recipe that a young chef in the kitchens of Le Gavroche cooked for me. We serve it in the restaurant for a little 'amuse-bouche' topped with a grilled prawn, but at home I make a big bowl to serve with any kind of grilled seafood. It is so good it can also be eaten on its own as a delicious summer salad.

Trim off the ends of the aubergines, cut lengthways into slices, about 15mm thick, then into cubes.

Heat a large, non-stick frying pan with a generous amount of vegetable oil. When the oil is smoking hot, add the aubergine cubes. They will soak up all the oil, but don't worry – carry on cooking over a high heat until the aubergine is lightly browned. Turn down the heat and gently simmer until tender. The whole cooking process should take about 12 minutes.

Season well with salt and chilli powder to taste. Remember, if the salad is to be served cold it will need more seasoning than if eaten warm. Put the aubergines in a colander and leave to drain for about 10 minutes.

Return the aubergines to the frying pan and heat gently. Fold in the ketchup, mustard and lemon juice. Simmer for 3–4 minutes, then remove and chill.

Just before serving, fold in the spring onions and toasted coconut chips.

Spicy Fresh Crab Salad

600g white crabmeat
1 large avocado, diced
2 spring onions, thinly sliced
juice of 2 limes
1 tablespoon sesame oil
salt
Tabasco sauce, to taste
200g brown crabmeat, pushed
  through a fine sieve
watercress, to garnish

Peppered tomato mousse
3 plum tomatoes, peeled,
  deseeded and chopped
pinch of sugar
1 teaspoon tomato purée
200ml whipping cream
1 tablespoon green peppercorns
  in brine, lightly crushed

Serves 6

The best way to cook a crab is to drown it first: just submerge it in cold fresh water for 5 minutes and it will gently pass away. Then cook it in boiling salted water for 18 minutes (for a large, 2kg crab). If all this together with the cracking and picking seems like too much work, buy the best-quality fresh picked claw meat — not frozen or pasteurised.

Put the white crabmeat in a bowl and add the avocado, spring onions, lime juice, sesame oil, salt and Tabasco. Mix gently with a fork, but do not overmix as you should keep the delicate flaky texture of the crabmeat.

Place a spoonful of the brown crab meat in each serving dish, then add the white meat mixture. Top with a small quenelle of peppered tomato mousse. Shape the quenelle by dipping 2 dessertspoons into hot water. Garnish with watercress.

Peppered tomato mousse

Put the chopped tomatoes and sugar in a pan over low heat, stirring occasionally, until all the moisture has evaporated and the tomatoes are thick. Leave to cool.

Add the tomato purée and pass through a fine sieve. Whip the cream until firm but not too stiff, then fold in the tomato mixture and the green peppercorns. Chill in the refrigerator until firm.

Pea and Broad Bean Salad with Fresh Mint and Scallops

200g fresh peas, shelled
200g fresh broad beans, shelled
1 bunch mint, coarsely chopped
2 spring onions, sliced
olive oil

salt and pepper
12 scallops with their coral
2 tablespoons sweet, well-aged
  balsamic vinegar

Serves 4

Blanch the peas and broad beans in a pan of boiling salted water, then plunge them into iced water to retain their vibrant green colour and halt the cooking. Keep them slightly underdone. Drain and remove the skins of the broad beans, which tend to be hard and bitter. Large peas could also be skinned. Add the mint, spring onions and 4 tablespoons of olive oil to the beans and peas and arrange the salad on the plates. Season with salt and pepper.

Smear a non-stick frying pan with olive oil and cook the scallops over a high heat until caramelised on both sides. They should take about 30 seconds each side, depending on their size. Season and arrange neatly on the salad. Drizzle over some balsamic vinegar and serve immediately.

Smoked Eel and Carrot Salad

2–3 carrots
salt and pepper
1 teaspoon light brown sugar
1 smoked eel, about 1.2kg
2 sprigs coriander
3 tablespoons groundnut oil

Horseradish cream
3 tablespoons double cream
2 tablespoons horseradish
1 spring onion, thinly sliced

Serves 6

Cut the carrots into very fine juliennes. Season with salt and pepper, then stir in the sugar and cover with clingfilm. Chill in the refrigerator for 12 hours.

If the eel has not been skinned or filleted, this is not such a daunting task as it may seem, certainly not as difficult as skinning live eels. Simply score the skin near the head and pull the skin towards the tail; it comes off as easily as peeling a banana! To fillet, use a thin-bladed knife and follow the backbone all the way down to the tail. Cut the eel fillets into neat diamond shapes (2cm wide) and set aside.

Take the carrots out of the refrigerator; they will have given off a golden-coloured liquid. Drain, reserving the liquid. Press the carrots into a ring (6cm in diameter by 4cm deep), then remove the ring and arrange the eel diamonds on top. Add a spoonful of the horseradish cream.

Blend the coriander leaves with the groundnut oil using a hand-held blender or in a mortar and pestle, then drizzle the coriander oil and the carrot juices on the plates to give a bright, vibrant, summer salad.

Horseradish cream

Whip the cream until stiff. Stir in the horseradish and spring onion and chill in the refrigerator until ready to serve.

Watercress and Pear Salad

6 bunches of watercress,
  about 50g per person
1 red onion
2 William pears
pepper

Sweet mustard dressing
1 tablespoon scented honey
1 tablespoon malt vinegar
a pinch of salt
2 tablespoons wholegrain
  mustard
4 tablespoons olive oil

Serves 6

Cut off and discard the thickest parts of the watercress stalks. Wash the rest well in ice-cold water, drain and spin dry. Thinly slice the onion. Peel the pears and slice into paper-thin curls with a Japanese vegetable slicer or a peeler. Be sure to do this at the last moment or the pear will discolour. Gently toss all the ingredients together with the mustard dressing and season well with pepper.

Sweet mustard dressing

Whisk the honey, malt vinegar, salt and mustard together, then gradually whisk in the olive oil. This recipe makes more than enough for the above salad, but the dressing can be stored for several weeks.

Asparagus Salad with Herb Vinaigrette and Bacon

8–12 asparagus spears
  per person
60g smoked bacon
  per person, cut into 20mm
  x3mm strips
extra virgin olive oil

2 thin slices of smoked bacon
  per person
red wine vinegar
salt and pepper
herb vinaigrette (see page 213)
fresh chervil, tarragon, and
  chives, to garnish

The oddly shaped purple asparagus from Provence is the tastiest, closely rivalled by the succulent tender green tips from Norfolk, England. Fat white asparagus can be strong and slightly bitter-tasting and is better if cooked for a little longer than its green cousins.

To peel the asparagus, lay the spears flat on a work surface and using a vegetable peeler, start peeling 3cm down from the tip. Some asparagus, especially the white variety, has two layers of skin, so make sure both are removed; the flesh should be white when peeled. Trim the asparagus to 9cm lengths, tie in bundles of ten, and cook in a pan of boiling salted water. Asparagus should not be overcooked. Refresh in ice-cold water, then drain.

Blanch the bacon strips by placing in cold water and bringing to the boil. Drain on kitchen paper, then fry in a little olive oil until they begin to turn golden and crisp. Grill the whole slices of bacon.

Roll the asparagus in a little extra virgin olive oil, vinegar, salt and pepper. Arrange on serving plates in a star shape, sprinkle the lardons over the asparagus and place two slices of grilled bacon on top. Finally, drizzle the herb vinaigrette around the plate and garnish with a few herbs.

Savoie Salad

6 salad potatoes (Charlotte, Belle de Fontenay), unpeeled
walnut oil
salt and pepper
olive oil, for frying
200g air-dried lightly smoked bacon, cut into 20mm x 5mm lardons

red wine vinegar
750g mâche salad (lamb's lettuce)
2 shallots, thinly sliced
300g Comte, Gruyère or Beaufort, shaved

Serves 6

Mâche salad grows in sandy soil and needs to be soaked in plenty of iced water before gently spinning to dry, it is a very tender leaf and needs to be handled with care or it will bruise and easily wilt.

Cook the potatoes in a large pan of boiling salted water until tender. Drain and leave to cool.

When the potatoes are cool enough to handle, peel and slice thinly, then drizzle with a little walnut oil. Season with salt and pepper, then cover and keep warm.

Heat a smear of olive oil in a pan and gently fry the lardons until crispy but not dry. Add a few drops of vinegar and pour all of this into the potatoes.

Dress the well-washed salad with a little walnut oil, vinegar and salt and pepper. Add the shallots and then the warm potato mix. Finally, sprinkle over the cheese shavings. Serve warm.

Roast Chicken Salad

1 leek, thinly sliced
salt and pepper
1 small corn fed chicken,
  about 1.3kg
olive oil
4 shallots, chopped
5 tablespoons extra virgin
  strong olive oil
125ml dry white wine
3 tablespoons balsamic vinegar

1 tablespoon honey
1 tablespoon wholegrain
  mustard
2 globe artichokes, trimmed
  to reveal the heart and chokes
  removed
500g mixed leaves
1 small baguette, cut into 24
  thin slices
1 garlic clove, cut in half

Serves 8

This recipe is for chicken, but can be done with other roasts, such as duck or beef and even leftover roasts, but most important is that the meat is served warm on the salad.

Preheat the oven to 190°C/Gas 5. Blanch the leek slices in a pan of boiling salted water for 30 seconds and refresh in iced water. Leave to drain. Rub the chicken with salt, pepper and a little olive oil and roast in the oven for 45 minutes until golden and cooked through. Remove the chicken from the roasting pan and leave to rest in a warm place.

Drain off some of the fat from the pan and add the shallots with 1 tablespoon of extra virgin olive oil. Cook for 2–3 minutes, stirring well. Add the wine, reduce by half and add any juices from the chicken. Take off the heat and whisk in the vinegar, honey, mustard and the remaining 4 tablespoons extra virgin olive oil. Set this vinaigrette aside.

Cut the trimmed artichokes into segments and pan-fry in a non-stick pan with a little olive oil until browned. Add the leeks to warm through and season well.

To serve, shred the chicken into bite-sized pieces while still warm. Toss the warm leeks and artichokes in a little of the vinaigrette and arrange on serving plates. Toss the mixed leaves and finally the chicken. Garnish with fried croûtons of baguette rubbed with the cut garlic clove.

Leek Salad Egg Vinaigrette

16 young leeks, washed
2 tablespoons Dijon mustard
2 tablespoons red wine vinegar
salt and pepper
4–6 tablespoons water

300ml vegetable or
 groundnut oil
2 eggs, hard-boiled and chopped
1 bunch chives, snipped

Serves 4

When leeks are young and tender, there can be no better way to enjoy them than in this simple French classic. This salad is perfect served with a selection of different meats and chunks of country-style bread.

Trim the dark green tops of the leeks, leaving about 3cm of the light green. Cook the leeks in a pan of boiling salted water for about 6 minutes or until tender. Drain and lay flat on a rack to cool while you make the vinaigrette.

Mix the mustard, vinegar and salt and pepper together in a bowl with a little of the water. Whisk as if making a mayonnaise, slowly adding the oil to emulsify the vinaigrette. Add a little more water if the mixture becomes too thick.

Cut the leeks in half lengthways and place in a serving dish or on a plate. Scatter over the chopped egg and snipped chives. Drizzle with the vinaigrette and eat before the leeks get cold.

Starters and Light Meals

Soft-boiled Egg with Smoked Salmon, Asparagus and Caviar

30 small asparagus tips
salt and pepper
4 slices smoked salmon
2 tablespoons double cream
2 tablespoons horseradish

4 eggs
3 tablespoons sevruga caviar
olive oil
12 round brioche bread toasts,
  about 1cm thick, 3–5cm wide

Serves 6

Peel the asparagus (page 71) and trim to 4cm lengths. Cook in a pan of boiling salted water for about 5–7 minutes or until just tender, then immediately refresh in ice-cold water and drain well.

Cut the smoked salmon slices into 18 circles, using a cutter the same diameter as the brioche.

Whip the cream and add to the horseradish.

Cook the eggs in boiling water for 3½ minutes, then hold under cold running water for 10 seconds, and peel while still hot. Put the eggs into a warm dish and break them up with a fork (the yolks should be runny and the whites solid). Season with a little pepper and gently fold in the caviar.

Reheat the asparagus in a pan of boiling salted water, drain and roll in a little olive oil to make them glossy.

Put a small dollop of horseradish cream in the centre of each serving plate, then a smoked salmon circle, more horseradish and then the lightly toasted brioche slice. Repeat the layers to finish with two brioches and three smoked salmon circles on each plate. Arrange the asparagus on top and spoon on the egg and caviar mixture.

Rare Peppered Tuna with Ginger and Sesame Dressing

480g tuna loin (preferably
  yellowfin)
1 tablespoon crushed black and
  white pepper
2 tablespoons sesame seeds
6cm piece of fresh ginger
1 tablespoon clear honey

6 tablespoons Japanese soy
  sauce
juice of 2 limes
2 tablespoons sesame oil
2 spring onions, sliced
1 medium hot red chilli, sliced

Serves 6

Preheat the grill, if using. Remove any dark parts from the bloodline on the tuna, then cut into manageable strips of about 4cm width.

Roll the strips in the pepper and press so they coat the tuna, then sear under the grill or in a non-stick pan on all sides for about 4 minutes to keep it very rare. Leave to cool slightly, then slice into ½cm thick slices and put in a serving dish.

To make the dressing, toast the sesame seeds and set aside. Cut the ginger into very fine juliennes.

Using a fork, mix the honey, soy sauce, lime juice and sesame oil together. Add the sesame seeds, ginger, spring onions and chilli. Serve with the tuna.

Tartare of Sea Bass with Dill

500g sea bass fillets
2 shallots, finely chopped
1 small bunch of dill, finely
    chopped

salt
3 tablespoons Greek yoghurt
juice of 1 lime
Green Tabasco sauce, to taste

Serves 6

The sea bass, needless to say, must be vey fresh. I prefer to use green Tabasco for this recipe as it is fragrant and not quite so strong. This must be seasoned at the last minute otherwise the fish will burn from the seasoning and change its texture.

Rinse the fish, then remove all bones and skin. Dice and put in a bowl set on ice.

Add the shallots and dill to the fish and season with salt. Fold in the yoghurt, lime juice, Tabasco and salt to taste.

Serve with hot toasted brown bread and a salad of Little Gem lettuce leaves dressed with a nut oil and lemon juice. If you are feeling extravagant, add a generous spoonful of caviar to each serving!

Gnocchi with Wild Mushroom Gratin

Choux pastry
250ml water
100g butter
a pinch of salt
a pinch of ground white pepper
1 teaspoon dry cep powder
 (optional)
125g plain flour, sifted
3 free-range eggs

Béchamel sauce
30g butter

30g plain flour
350ml milk
salt and pepper
grated nutmeg
1 sprig thyme and 1 bay leaf

Filling and topping
360g mixed wild mushrooms
olive oil
2 garlic cloves, crushed
60g Cheddar, grated
40g Parmesan, grated

Serves 4–6

Start by making the choux pastry. Bring the water and butter to the boil with the seasoning. As soon as it boils, take the pan off the heat and stir in the flour with a spatula. When this is well mixed and smooth, return the pan to the heat. Cook the choux pastry over a medium heat for 2–3 minutes, stirring vigorously all the time. Take off the heat and beat in the eggs one at a time. Put the choux paste in a piping bag with an 8mm hole. Gently squeeze the bag over a pan of boiling salted water, and using a small, sharp knife, cut the paste into roughly 1cm lengths as it comes out. Simmer the gnocchi for 5 minutes, then gently lift them out with a slotted spoon. Put them straight into iced water to halt the cooking, then drain in a colander.

Next make the béchamel. Melt the butter in a saucepan, add the flour and cook until foaming, but do not allow to colour. Slowly whisk in the milk over a high heat and add the seasoning and herbs. Bring to the boil, then turn the heat down and simmer for 10 minutes. Take off the heat, pour through a fine sieve, cover and set aside.

Preheat the oven to 200°C/Gas 6. Pan-fry the mushrooms in a little olive oil, allowing them to colour a little. Add the garlic and season with salt and a little pepper. Scatter the gnocchi and mushrooms into an ovenproof dish, about 20cm x 28cm and 5cm deep, or some individual dishes. Pour over the béchamel sauce and sprinkle with the cheese. Bake in the oven for 20 minutes until golden brown.

Creamy Crab Gratin

400g picked crabmeat	salt and pepper
4 shallots, finely chopped	grated nutmeg
4 tablespoons port	120ml crème fraîche
2 egg yolks	50g Parmesan, freshly grated

Serves 4

Serve these delicious little pots with toasted sourdough bread as a starter or make in a large dish as a rather rich and luxurious main course. Try to use only crab claw meat for this dish if you can.

Preheat the oven to 180°C/Gas 4. Gently mix the crab with all the other ingredients except the Parmesan, fold in the seasoning and then divide the mixture between four ovenproof ramekin dishes or similar.

Sprinkle the Parmesan on top and bake in the oven for 8–10 minutes. If the cheese has not browned, place under a preheated hot grill for a few seconds.

Baked Eggs with Ham and Truffle

1 truffle, about 40g
4 thin slices Parma ham
200ml crème fraîche

salt and pepper
4 free-range eggs

Serves 4

Truffles are an extravagant luxury but well worth saving up for. Make sure you buy the most fragrant, ripe, winter truffles. The black Périgord truffle is usually at its best from January to March and should be tender to touch and jet black. Place it in an airtight container with the eggs and keep chilled for at least 3 days before using. As the shells of eggs are porous, they will take on the scent of the truffle.

Using a pastry brush, butter four ovenproof glass or porcelain ramekin dishes, large and deep enough to take an egg and 2 tablespoons of crème fraîche.

Preheat the oven to 150°C/Gas 2. Slice the truffle thinly using a small, sharp knife or a truffle slicer. Carefully place the truffle slices around the inside of each dish. Cut the Parma ham slices into strips and put a little in each dish. Add a spoonful of crème fraîche, more Parma ham, any truffle that's left over, and then the remaining crème fraîche. Season lightly, then carefully break an egg on top of the crème fraîche in each ramekin.

Place the ramekins in a bain-marie and bake in the oven for about 10 minutes. The whites of the eggs should be set and the yolks still a little runny. Finish with a sprinkle of salt and pepper and serve with some toasted brioche.

Mushroom Soufflé

350g mushrooms, preferably
  mixed wild mushrooms:
  chanterelles, field, parasol
30g butter
juice of ½ lemon
1 tablespoon double cream
salt and pepper
grated nutmeg
1 teaspoon cornflour, dissolved
  in 2 teaspoons cold water

4 eggs, separated
1 tablespoon Parmesan,
  freshly grated

Mushroom sauce (optional)
80g button mushrooms, sliced
1 tablespoon butter
125ml chicken stock (page 208)
250ml double cream
salt and pepper

Serves 4

Preheat the oven to 200°C/Gas 6. Butter four individual soufflé dishes, about 9cm in diameter.

Cut the mushrooms into quarters, then place in a saucepan with the butter and lemon juice and cook over a medium heat for 10 minutes. Add the cream and bring to the boil. Season with salt, pepper and nutmeg, then purée in a blender until smooth.

Return the mixture to the pan and add the dissolved cornflour. Cook over a high heat, whisking continuously, until thick. Take the pan off the heat, add the egg yolks and whisk until smooth.

Whisk the egg whites until they form soft peaks, then fold them into the warm mixture. Divide between the buttered soufflé dishes, sprinkle with Parmesan and cook in the oven for 10 minutes.

Serve immediately. If you wish, you can make a mushroom sauce to be poured into the soufflés at the table.

Mushroom sauce

Sweat the mushrooms in the butter for 3–4 minutes. Add the stock and reduce by half, then add the cream and reduce by a third. Season with salt and pepper, then purée in a blender. Finally, pass through a fine sieve.

Soufflé Suissesse

45g butter
45g plain flour
500ml milk
5 egg yolks
salt and white pepper

6 egg whites
600ml double cream
200g Gruyère or Emmental
  cheese, grated

Serves 4

Preheat the oven to 200°C/Gas 6. Butter four 8cm diameter tartlet moulds.

Melt the butter in a heavy-based pan, whisk in the flour and cook, stirring continuously, for about 1 minute. Whisk in the milk and boil for 3 minutes, whisking all the time to prevent any lumps from forming. Beat in the egg yolks and take off the heat. Season with salt and pepper, then cover with a piece of buttered greaseproof paper to prevent a skin from forming.

Whisk the egg whites with a pinch of salt until they form firm, but not stiff, peaks. Add a third of the egg whites to the yolk mixture and beat with a whisk until evenly mixed, then gently fold in the remaining egg whites. Spoon the mixture into the well-buttered tartlet moulds and cook in the oven for 3 minutes or until the tops begin to turn golden.

Meanwhile, season the cream with a little salt, warm it gently and pour into a gratin dish. Turn the soufflés out into the cream, sprinkle the grated cheese over the soufflés, then return to the oven for 5 minutes. Serve immediately.

Moules Marinière

3kg mussels
1 large onion, finely chopped
4 celery sticks, finely chopped
1 garlic clove, finely chopped
1 tablespoon butter

400ml dry white wine
200g crème fraîche
1 bunch of flat leaf parsley
salt and pepper

Serves 4

I don't think there can be a better way to enjoy mussels, with a steaming creamy broth to dunk a piece of fresh bread in and a glass of Muscadet wine, this is the ubiquitous French brasserie classic.

Wash and scrape the mussels, discarding any broken ones. Sweat the onion, celery and garlic in the butter in a large, tall saucepan. Pour in the wine and bring to a rapid boil. Add the mussels and cover.

After 3 minutes shake the pan and stir the mussels. Cover again and continue to cook for about 7–8 minutes or until all the mussels have opened.

Remove the mussels with a slotted spoon and put them in a large tureen or individual deep bowls. Continue to boil the liquid in the pan. Add the crème fraîche, chopped parsley and seasoning, and as soon as the liquid has come back to the boil, pour it over the mussels. Serve at once.

Red Onion, Fennel and Chilli Tarte Tatin

220g puff pastry
6 red onions, sliced into thick rounds
3 fennel bulbs, cut into 6 pieces
4 mild red chillies
100ml olive oil
2 tablespoons balsamic vinegar
salt and pepper
1 teaspoon coriander seeds, crushed
60g caster sugar
3 tablespoons water
2 teaspoons thyme leaves
3 garlic cloves, crushed
150g Parmesan, freshly grated

Serves 4

A great vegetarian dish for all to enjoy, the sweetness of the red onions with the bite of the chilli make this a perfect starter or main.

Preheat the oven to 190°C/Gas 5. Roll out the pastry to a circle large enough to cover a tart tin or tatin dish about 28cm in diameter. Leave to rest in the refrigerator until needed.

Put the onions, fennel and chillies into a roasting pan, pour over the olive oil, vinegar, salt, pepper and coriander seeds and roast in the oven for 30 minutes, turning occasionally but being careful to keep the onion rings in one piece.

In a separate pan or directly in a tatin dish, mix the sugar and water together. Quickly bring to the boil, then continue to cook without stirring until golden brown. Take off the heat and pour into the base of the tart tin if you have used a separate pan.

Turn the oven up to 200°C/Gas 6. Arrange all the vegetables in a decorative pattern in the tin and press down tightly. Sprinkle with the thyme, garlic and Parmesan. Cover with the puff pastry and tuck in at the edges between the vegetables and the sides of the tin. Prick the pastry with a fork and bake in the oven for 30–40 minutes until the puff pastry is golden and fully cooked. Leave to cool for at least 20 minutes before turning upside down onto a serving dish.

Pumpkin and Swede Crumble

100g butter, cold
150g plain flour, sifted
1 heaped teaspoon sea salt
100g Cheddar cheese, grated
75g almonds, hazelnuts or
 walnuts, chopped
300g pumpkin
300g swede
300g butternut squash
 (peeled weight)
2 tablespoons olive oil
1 medium onion, chopped

salt and pepper
grated nutmeg
2 sprigs rosemary
2 garlic cloves, finely chopped

Balsamic dressing
30ml balsamic vinegar
1 teaspoon demerara sugar
2 tablespoons olive oil
1 tablespoon Dijon
 wholegrain mustard

Serves 6–8

This is a delicious winter dish which needs no accompaniment – it is a meal itself. The crumble can be made in advance and stored in an airtight container in the fridge. The pumpkin mix can also be made beforehand and sprinkled with the crumble before baking.

For the crumble topping, work the butter into the flour using your fingertips, then gently rub between your hands to obtain a sandy, coarse crumb. Add the salt, cheese and nuts, but do not overmix. The texture should stay very loose and sandy. Set aside.

Preheat the oven to 180°C/Gas 4. Cut the pumpkin, swede and squash into bite-sized chunks and place in a heavy-based pan with the olive oil. Cook over a high heat, stirring occasionally, until the vegetables start to take on a little colour. Turn the heat down to medium and add the onion, seasoning and rosemary. Cover with foil and cook for 20 minutes or until tender. Now stir in the garlic and continue to cook for a further 10 minutes.

Discard the rosemary and pour the vegetables into an ovenproof dish. This should have a depth of 4cm and be large enough to take all the mixture. Sprinkle the crumble mix over the vegetables and bake in the oven for 20 minutes until crisp and golden.

For the dressing, mix all the ingredients together, then serve with the crumble.

Poached Scallops with Leeks and Smoked Salmon

1 large leek
salt and pepper
150ml water
6 very large scallops, about
  80g each
3 tablespoons Chardonnay wine
100ml double cream

120g unsalted butter, cubed
juice of 1 lemon
grated zest of ½ lemon
3 thin slices of smoked salmon,
  cut into very thin strips
sevruga caviar, to garnish
  (optional)

Serves 6

It can be difficult to find large scallops because of overfishing, but you can use 12 or 18 smaller scallops if big ones are not available. If you would like to prepare them yourself, buy them in the shell, ensuring they are alive. Scallops should always be diver caught, not dredged, and should be fresh, not soaked in water.

Remove the outside leaf of the leek and set aside. Cut the white, yellow, and tender green parts into 6cm x 1cm strips. Blanch in a pan of boiling salted water until cooked but still a little crunchy. Refresh in ice-cold water and drain well.

Chop the outer green leaf of the leek and place in a pan with the leek trimmings. Add the water and boil for 5 minutes. Pass through a sieve and set the stock aside.

Put the scallops and wine into a wide saucepan over a medium heat, season lightly with salt and pepper and bring to a simmer. Add enough of the leek stock to come three-quarters of the way up the scallops. Turn the scallops and continue to cook for 2 minutes. For my taste, scallops are best cooked rare, otherwise they lose their flavour and delicate texture.

Remove the scallops from the pan and set aside. Add the cream and whisk in the butter. Add the leeks to the sauce with the lemon juice and zest. Serve the leek ribbons and scallops with the strips of smoked salmon on top. If you are feeling extravagant – and I recommend it – a generous spoonful of sevruga caviar finishes the dish perfectly.

Spicy Crab Cakes

500g crab claw meat
2 shallots, chopped
1 sprig coriander, chopped
1 sprig opal basil
2 dried chillies, chopped
60g Japanese breadcrumbs
   (Panko), plus extra for dusting
juice of ½ lemon
salt and pepper
1 teaspoon sugar
1 egg

2 tablespoons Dijon mustard
4 tablespoons mayonnaise
lime wedges, to serve

Ginger and spring onion
crème fraîche
50g piece of fresh ginger, peeled
125g crème fraîche
3 spring onions, sliced
juice of 1 lemon
green Tabasco sauce, to taste

Serves 8

Make sure the crab is clean without any bones or cartilage. Mix the chopped shallots, coriander, basil and chillies together and add to the crab. Gently fold in the breadcrumbs, lemon juice, seasoning, sugar, egg, mustard and mayonnaise, then leave to chill in the refrigerator for 1 hour.

Press the mixture into small cakes about 2cm deep and dust with the extra Japanese breadcrumbs.

Heat a little vegetable oil in a non-stick pan and pan-fry the crab cakes in batches until golden on both sides. Serve with lime wedges and salad and the ginger and spring onion crème fraîche on the side.

Ginger and spring onion crème fraîche

Dice the ginger very finely – a Japanese vegetable slicer helps. Fold the ginger into the crème fraîche with the sliced spring onions and season to taste with salt, pepper, lemon juice and Green Tabasco.

Tagliatelle with Green Olive Paste and Bayonne Ham

8 slices of Bayonne ham (or air
  dried ham such as Parma ham)
300g dried tagliatelle
salt and pepper
few sprigs thyme, to garnish

Green olive paste
2 red peppers
100g good-quality green olives
  (not in brine), pitted
5 tablespoons olive oil
1 tablespoon thyme, leaves only

Serves 4

Shred the ham. Boil the pasta in a large pan of boiling salted water until *al dente*.

Drain the pasta, return to the pan and toss in the olive paste. Add the shreds of ham, garnish with a few sprigs of thyme and serve immediately with freshly ground black pepper.

Green olive paste

Char, skin and dice the peppers. Blend the olives with the olive oil until the mixture is paste-like but not smooth. Mix in the peppers and thyme leaves. This makes more than you need for the pasta, but it keeps well in the refrigerator.

Hot Goat's Cheese Pies

500g plain flour
60ml strong olive oil
140ml water
pinch of salt
16 black olives marinated in oil

16 green olives marinated in oil
16 Rocamadour cheeses
2 garlic cloves, chopped
1 bunch basil
1 egg, beaten

Serves 8

Rocamadour cheeses are almost small enough to pop into your mouth whole and are perfect for making into these little pies. Cheese that is a little dry is best for this recipe. These pies make a great starter to any dinner party.

Sift the flour into a bowl. Make a well in the centre, add the olive oil, salt and water, then bring the dough together using your fingertips. Do not overwork. Wrap in clingfilm and leave to chill in the refrigerator for 1 hour.

Roll out the dough using a pasta roller. Place 8 rings, measuring 5cm x 2cm, on a baking sheet. Cut the dough into circles 8cm across and line each ring – you'll find you have a little more dough than you need.

Preheat the oven to 190°C/Gas 5. Chop all the olives. Place a Rocamadour cheese in each lined ring. Add a spoonful of chopped olives and garlic, then a couple of basil leaves. Place another Rocamadour cheese on top of the olives, followed by a couple more basil leaves. Bring the overlapping pastry over the cheese and seal well by pressing and moistening with a little water. Turn the pies over so that the seal is underneath. Brush with the beaten egg and score with the point of a knife to decorate. Bake in the oven for 15–20 minutes until golden.

Pilau Rice with Beaufort

1 tablespoon sultanas
1 onion, chopped
2 tablespoons butter
1 teaspoon cumin seeds
2 sprigs thyme
1 bay leaf
200g long-grain rice

½ litre chicken stock (page 208)
12 fresh walnuts
200g Beaufort, shaved
salt and pepper
1 mountain sausage, about 200g,
    skinned and thinly sliced

Serves 4

Look for an old Beaufort made from the summer pastures. Alternatively, you could use a mature Cheddar. The mountain sausage is a dry, thin salami made from pork. If you would like to serve some wine with this then Vin d'arbois is an excellent choice, as it is from the same region as the Beaufort.

Preheat the oven to 190°C/Gas 5. Put the sultanas in a pan, cover with cold water and bring to a simmer for 2 minutes, then drain and set aside.

Sweat the onion in 1 tablespoon of the butter in a wide pan until soft but not coloured. Add the cumin, thyme, bay leaf and rice. Stir to coat the rice, then cook for 2–3 minutes. Pour in the stock, bring to the boil, then cover with greaseproof paper and cook in the oven for 16–18 minutes.

Take out of the oven and remove the paper. All the liquid should have been absorbed and the rice should be just cooked. With a fork, gently fluff up the rice and mix in the walnuts, sultanas, remaining butter and half of the cheese. Season to taste. Place in a hot bowl and sprinkle with the sausage and remaining cheese.

Chilli Coconut Fried Tiger Prawns

24 raw tiger prawns
250g desiccated coconut
2–3 dried red chillies or more
  to taste, chopped

salt and pepper
200g cornflour
3 egg whites
vegetable oil, for deep-frying

Serves 8

These are delicious cooked either on the barbecue or simply pan-fried in a non-stick pan without any fat; they can even be cooked under a hot grill. I often use this recipe for canapés at Le Gavroche but once you get the taste for them you just can't stop.

Remove the heads and shells from the prawns, leaving the tails intact, then devein to remove the intestines.

Spread the desiccated coconut and chopped chillies out on a plate and season with salt and pepper. Spread the cornflour out on another plate and put the egg whites in a bowl and beat lightly.

Dip the prawns into the cornflour and then into the beaten egg whites. Finally coat in the seasoned coconut and chilli.

Deep-fry the prawns until golden brown, then drain on kitchen paper and serve piping hot.

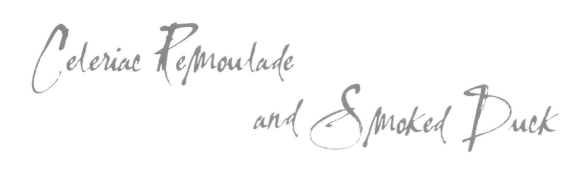

Celeriac Remoulade and Smoked Duck

2 egg yolks
½ tablespoon Dijon mustard
juice of 1 lemon
salt and pepper
200ml vegetable oil

1 celeriac, about 500g
1 tablespoon grain mustard
2 mini baguettes
1 smoked duck supreme
2 spring onions, thinly sliced

Serves 6

This is an all time French classic and is great on its own or served with cold cuts. I always find it better a day or two after it's been made, when the flavours and textures have had time to mature.

Start by making the mayonnaise. Whisk together the egg yolks, Dijon mustard, lemon juice and salt and pepper. Gradually whisk in the vegetable oil until all the oil is incorporated and the mixture is completely emulsified.

Peel the celeriac, taking care to remove enough of the skin as it can be woody. Using a vegetable slicer, cut the celeriac into very fine julienne strips. Add these to the mayonnaise and stir in the mustard. Leave to stand for at least a couple of hours so the celeriac has time to soften.

Slice the baguettes into about 30 bite-sized slices and toast on both sides. Remove some of the fat from the duck and slice very thinly to make at least 30 pieces. Twirl a little remoulade on to each toast with a fork, add a strip of duck on top and garnish with some sliced spring onions.

Spaghetti with Razor Clams, Parsley and Garlic

1kg fresh live razor clams
2 shallots, finely chopped
4 tablespoons olive oil
200ml dry white wine
300g dried spaghetti

1 bunch flat leaf parsley
2 garlic cloves, chopped
1–2 red chillies to taste,
  chopped
salt and pepper

Serves 4

Make sure your razor clams are alive and bought from a reputable fishmonger. If you can't get razor clams, use a mixture of clams such as Venus, Surf, Amande or Palourde instead. You can also use fresh spaghetti, if you wish.

Rinse the razor clams in cold water. Sweat the shallots in a large pan with ½ tablespoon of olive oil. Add the clams and turn up the heat. Pour in the wine and cover tightly. After 3 or 4 minutes, shake the pan and check the clams. The exact time they take to cook will depend on the variety used.

As soon as all the clams are open, take the pan off the heat – they go chewy if overcooked. Drain into a colander set over a bowl to collect all the juices. Pick out the flesh of the clams – leave a few in their shells for the garnish – and remove the little sand bag or intestine at the base of each meaty mollusc. Pass the cooking juices through a fine sieve and boil until reduced by half.

Cook the pasta in a large pan of boiling salted water until *al dente*, then drain and return to the pan. In another pan, reheat the clams in the reduced juice and add the oil, chopped parsley, garlic and chillies. Pour this mixture into the pasta and toss everything together. Check for seasoning, then garnish each bowl with some clams in the shell and serve immediately.

Blinis with Caviar

15g fresh yeast or 1 sachet dry
200ml warm milk
50g wholemeal flour
3 eggs
75g strong white flour
75g rye flour
pinch of salt
vegetable oil, for cooking

Garnish
125ml whipping cream
125ml crème fraîche
200g (or more!) caviar
4 spring onions, sliced into thin
  slivers

Makes 20 pieces

First make the blinis. Dissolve the yeast in the warm milk, then mix in the wholemeal flour, cover and leave to ferment in a draught-free place for 1 hour.

Meanwhile mix 1 whole egg and 2 egg yolks with the remaining flours and the salt, then cover and leave for 1 hour. Mix with the fermenting dough.

Whisk the remaining 2 egg whites until stiff, then fold into the mixture.

Heat a non-stick pan with a drop of vegetable oil. Drop a spoonful of the mixture into the pan and cook for a minute or two, then flip over to cook the other side. Continue until all the mixture is used up.

Garnish

For the garnish, whip the cream until it forms peaks, then fold into the crème fraîche. Pipe or spoon the mixture on to each blini, then spoon on a generous amount of caviar and add a sliver of spring onion.

Potato and Gruyère Soufflés

400g large potatoes
  (Maris Piper or Desirée)
100ml double cream
250g Gruyère cheese, grated
2 eggs

salt and pepper
grated nutmeg
50 cooked puff pastry tartlet
  shells (4cm in diameter)

Makes 50 tartlets

Bake the potatoes in their skins, then leave until cool enough to handle. Preheat the oven to 190°C/Gas 5.

Bring the cream to the boil. Put the potato flesh into the bowl of an electric mixer, add the Gruyère and eggs, and beat for 30 seconds. Pour in the boiling cream, season to taste with salt, pepper and nutmeg, then beat for a further 30 seconds or so, until there are no more lumps (you may have to scrape down the sides of the bowl to make sure the mixture is smooth).

Put the mixture into a piping bag fitted with a plain nozzle and pipe into the pastry tartlets. Bake in the oven for about 2 minutes until lightly souffléd and golden brown. Serve at once.

Crispy Gruyère Pancakes

6 sheets of brique pastry
olive oil
120g Gruyère, grated
1 tablespoon crème fraîche
40g wild rocket leaves, chopped
2 spring onions, sliced
salt and pepper
chives

Crème fraîche vinaigrette
1 tablespoon crème fraîche
1 tablespoon olive oil
juice of 1 lemon
1 tablespoon water

Serves 4

These crispy pancakes should be served as soon as they are cooked and can make a good starter or cheese course. Brique pastry is a North Afican pancake, now available at good delis, but you could use spring roll sheets.

Preheat the oven to 180°C/Gas 4. Lay 4 sheets of the brique pastry on a flat work surface. Lightly brush with olive oil. Cut 4 smaller squares from the remaining brique and place these in the centre of each sheet to help support the filling. Brush with oil.

Mix the Gruyère and crème fraîche together. Add the rocket leaves together with the spring onions and lightly season the mixture. Divide the mixture between the sheets of brique. Bring the edges together and tie each parcel with a chive. Trim the tops slightly with scissors and brush again with a little olive oil. Bake in the oven for 8–10 minutes until golden and crisp.

These pancakes are ideal served with a little rocket salad seasoned with the crème fraîche vinaigrette and garnished with shavings of Gruyère.

Crème fraîche vinaigrette

Put all the ingredients in a bowl and mix together. Season to taste.

Dill and Crab Pancakes

500g crab claw meat
1 bunch of dill, roughly chopped
2 shallots, finely chopped
mayonnaise, tomato ketchup, brandy, to taste
Tabasco sauce, to taste
3 eggs
100g plain flour

6 tablespoons wholemeal flour
225ml milk
250ml water
1 tablespoon chopped dill
salt and pepper
vegetable oil, for cooking

Makes 16 pancakes;
6–8 canapés per pancake

To make the pancakes, beat the eggs with a whisk and gradually beat in the flours, milk, water, dill and seasoning. Pass through a coarse sieve and leave to rest for at least 1 hour.

Heat a small non-stick frying pan about 18cm in diameter. Brush lightly with vegetable oil and pour in just enough batter to coat the base of the pan. Cook over a medium-high heat, then flip over using a palette knife, and cook the other side. Stack the pancakes between sheets of greaseproof paper and leave to cool.

Pick through the crab meat to remove any bones and pieces of shell, then mix with the dill, shallots and mayonnaise, adding ketchup, brandy and Tabasco to taste. Spread the crab mixture over the pancakes and roll up to form cigar shapes. Trim the edges and place in the refrigerator until needed. Using a very sharp knife, slice into bite-sized pieces.

Fish and Shellfish

Roast Gilt-head Bream with Citrus Fruit Vinaigrette

4 gilt-head bream
  (400–500g each)
1 orange
1 lemon
1 pink grapefruit
salt and pepper

4 tablespoons extra virgin
  olive oil
2 shallots, finely chopped
2 sprigs basil, leaves only,
  shredded

Serves 4

Preheat the oven to 220°C/Gas 7. Scale the fish and remove the eyes and gills. Slit the belly and remove the guts. Rinse well under cold running water and pat dry with kitchen paper.

Peel the fruit and segment, removing all the pith, holding the fruit over a bowl to collect the juices.

Slash the skin of the fish three times on each side, and season with salt and pepper. Cook in a non-stick ovenproof pan with a drop of olive oil over a high heat to crisp the skin, turning the fish after 3 minutes. When both sides are browned, place in the oven for about 5 minutes, depending on the size of the fish.

Take the fish out of the pan and place them on plates or a serving dish to keep warm. Put the shallots in the same pan with 1 tablespoon of the olive oil and cook briskly for 1 minute. Add the fruit juices and reduce by a third; pour in any juices from the fish. Add the fruit segments and the remaining olive oil, then immediately take the pan off the heat and pour over the fish. Sprinkle with the basil leaves and serve; this should be warm, not hot.

Roast Salmon with Spicy Chorizo and Aïoli

6–8 new potatoes (Charlotte,
  Belle de Fontenay)
250g shelled broad beans
6 Little Gem lettuces
600ml veal stock (page 206)
2 teaspoons caster sugar

salt and pepper
olive oil
6 salmon pieces,
  about 175g each, skin on
30 thin slices spicy chorizo
aïoli (page 210), to serve

Serves 6

Preheat the oven to 180°C/Gas 4. Cook the potatoes in a pan of salted water until tender. Drain, peel, cut into thick slices and keep warm.

Cook the broad beans in a pan of boiling salted water until tender. Refresh in ice-cold water, then remove the outer skins to reveal the tender bright green beans.

Blanch the lettuces in a pan of boiling salted water for 3 minutes. Refresh in ice-cold water and squeeze dry. Put the lettuces in a wide pan with the stock, sugar, salt and pepper and boil until the stock has thickened enough to coat the lettuce lightly, baste the lettuce frequently as it cooks. Keep warm.

Heat a non-stick frying pan until very hot. Add a drop of olive oil and cook the salmon, skin side down, until browned. Turn over and cook the other side; this should take no more than 2–3 minutes on each side. The skin should be crispy yet the fish should remain very pink.

Warm the potato slices, broad beans and chorizo in the oven for 2 minutes.

To serve, put a lettuce in the centre of each plate with some of its cooking liquid. Arrange the broad beans, chorizo and potato slices around the lettuce, drizzle generously with the aïoli, then lay the salmon, skin side up, on top of the lettuce.

Roast Turbot with Grain Mustard and Tomatoes

6 thick turbot pieces, 160g each
salt and pepper
1 tablespoon olive oil
3 shallots, chopped
2 tablespoons dry white wine
1 tablespoon Dijon
  grain mustard
2 tablespoons chopped parsley
6 plum tomatoes, peeled,
  deseeded and diced

Beurre blanc
60ml dry white wine
2 teaspoons white wine vinegar
2 small shallots, finely chopped
2 tablespoons double cream
150g cold unsalted butter,
  cubed
salt and pepper

Serves 6

Season the turbot lightly with salt and pepper. Heat a large non-stick frying pan until very hot. Add the olive oil and cook the fish over a high heat for about 2 minutes, then turn and cook the other side for a further 2–3 minutes. Remove from the pan, cover with greaseproof paper and keep warm; any juices that come out of the fish can be poured into the sauce.

With the pan still on high heat, add the shallots and cook for 30 seconds, stirring so they don't burn, then pour in the wine and reduce by half. Whisk in the beurre blanc and the remaining ingredients, but do not allow to boil.

Serve the fish on a bed of baby spinach, cooked with a little olive oil until just wilted, and pour the sauce around.

Beurre blanc

Put the wine, vinegar and shallots in a heavy-based pan, bring to the boil and reduce by half. Add the cream and boil for 1 minute. Lower the heat and gradually whisk in the butter. Pass through a fine sieve and season with salt and pepper.

Roast John Dory, Artichokes Barigoule

1 John Dory, about 1kg
2 tablespoons olive oil
2 sprigs each of thyme
  and rosemary
salt

Artichokes barigoule
6 baby artichokes, preferably
  the variety called 'violets'
1 lemon, cut in half
75ml olive oil

2 slices of Bayonne or
  Parma ham, diced
½ small fennel bulb, diced
½ carrot, diced
½ onion, diced
1 garlic clove, chopped
1 teaspoon thyme leaves
200ml dry white wine
salt and coarsely ground pepper
60ml warm water
12 basil leaves, shredded

Serves 2

Preheat the oven to 220°C/Gas 7. Scale and fillet the fish, and remove any pin bones. Rinse under cold water and pat dry with kitchen paper. Score the skin several times with a sharp knife to prevent the fish from curling during cooking.

Heat a non-stick ovenproof pan until smoking hot. Add the olive oil, thyme and rosemary, then add the fish, skin side down, season with salt and cook over a high heat for 2 minutes. Place in the hot oven for 5 minutes. Using a spatula, gently turn the fish over and return to the oven for 3 minutes.

Artichokes barigoule

Trim the artichokes by cutting off the outer leaves and peeling the stalk. As you peel, rub the artichokes with a lemon half to prevent discolouring.

Heat a heavy-based saucepan, add 2 tablespoons of olive oil and cook the ham until starting to brown, stirring frequently. Add the vegetables, garlic and thyme, and cook for a further 5 minutes, stirring constantly.

Add the artichokes to the pan together with the wine, the juice of ½ lemon and salt and pepper. Bring to the boil, then pour in the water, cover loosely with greaseproof paper and cook for about 12 minutes or until the artichokes are tender, turning occasionally to ensure even cooking. Just before serving with the fish, mix in the remaining olive oil and basil leaves.

Roast Fillet of Sea Bass, Parsnip Purée, Caramelised Garlic

2 sea bass, 600g each
olive oil
3 shallots, sliced
80g button mushrooms, sliced
1 tablespoon white wine vinegar
100ml dry white wine
400ml veal stock (page 208)
salt and pepper
1 tablespoon butter

Caramelised garlic
8 small shallots
20 garlic cloves
olive oil

Parsnip purée
5 parsnips
120ml milk
1 tablespoon butter
salt and pepper

Parsnip crisps
1 parsnip
oil for deep-frying

Serves 4

Scale and fillet the fish, and remove any pin bones. Rinse under cold water and pat dry with kitchen paper. Score the skin of the fish several times with a sharp knife to help prevent the fish from curling during cooking. Leave the bones (not the heads) to soak in cold water.

To make the sauce, heat a little olive oil in a pan and cook the shallots for about 5 minutes until golden and soft. Add the mushrooms and continue to cook for 10 minutes, stirring occasionally. Drain the fish bones, add to the pan and cook for 5–6 minutes. Add the vinegar and wine and let it come to the boil for 3 minutes, then add the stock, season lightly and simmer for 30 minutes, skimming at regular intervals. Pass through a fine sieve into a clean pan, bring back to the boil and whisk in the butter to thicken and gloss the sauce.

Heat a non-stick frying pan until smoking hot, add a few drops of olive oil, then add the fish, skin side down. Season with salt and pepper and press the fish down with a palette knife if it begins to curl up. Once the skin is well browned, turn the fillets over and cook the other side; the whole process should not take more than 5–6 minutes, depending on the thickness of the fish.

Caramelised garlic

Peel the shallots and garlic. Blanch the shallots in boiling salted water for 10 minutes or until tender. Cut them in half if large and drain well. Put the garlic in a small saucepan of boiling salted water, bring to the boil for 2 minutes, then drain and change the water. Repeat 4 times and drain well. Heat a little olive oil in a frying pan over a medium heat, add the shallots and garlic and cook until caramelised, shaking the pan so they don't stick.

Parsnip purée

Peel the parsnips and cut them into big chunks. Cook in boiling salted water until tender. Bring the milk to the boil and set aside. Drain the parsnips well, then put in a blender with the butter and some of the boiled milk and blend until totally smooth: the purée should be the consistency of double cream, so add more milk if necessary. Season and keep warm.

Parsnip crisps

Peel the parsnip and slice lengthways, using a mandolin to slice it as thinly as possible. Deep-fry in hot oil until crisp. Drain on kitchen towels to absorb any excess fat and set aside in a dry place.

To serve, spoon the parsnip purée on to warmed plates, make a hollow in the centre, and fill with the caramelised garlic and shallots. Pour the sauce around the purée, place the fish on top and add a few parsnip crisps for garnish.

Red Mullet with an Orange Almond Crust

3 red mullet, 400g each
120g butter, softened
2 tablespoons white dry
  breadcrumbs
2 tablespoons ground almonds
2 teaspoons thyme leaves,
  chopped
1 tablespoon parsley, chopped
1 tablespoon coarsely cracked

black and white pepper
grated zest and juice
  of 1 orange
3 tomatoes
3 courgettes
olive oil
salt and pepper
juice of 1 lemon
1 small bunch basil

Serves 6

Red mullet is a very versatile fish and here I have teamed it with Mediterranean flavours. If serving this dish as part of a dinner party then try serving a fragrant Sancerre red wine or even a Bellet rosé, as these wines work very well with this fish.

Scale and fillet the fish, and remove any pin bones. Rinse under cold water and pat dry with kitchen paper. Place the fillets on a lightly oiled and seasoned baking tray.

Whisk the butter and add the breadcrumbs, ground almonds, thyme, parsley, pepper and the orange juice and zest. Leave to set in the refrigerator for 10 minutes.

Blanch the tomatoes in boiling water, refresh under cold water and remove the skins. Cut in half, deseed, roughly chop and set aside. Slice the courgettes and put them in a pan with a little olive oil. Season well and cook until lightly coloured but still crunchy. Add the tomatoes so they just warm through. Add the lemon juice and a little more olive oil and toss in the basil leaves.

Preheat the oven to 200°C/Gas 6. Make the almond paste into shapes the same size as your mullet fillets and place one on top of each piece of fish. Bake in the oven for 4 minutes and then put under a preheated hot grill to finish off cooking and to give the crust a golden-brown colour. Divide the tomato and courgette mixture between the plates and serve the fish on top.

Grilled Red Mullet
on Pea and Tomato Risotto

4 red mullet fillets, 150g each
125ml double cream
100g frozen petits pois
salt and pepper
500ml chicken stock (page 206)
butter
½ onion, chopped
200g arborio rice

150ml dry white wine
100g cooked fresh peas
2 tablespoons Parmesan, grated
olive oil
16 dried tomato halves, diced
(page 213)
balsamic vinegar
2 sprigs tarragon

Serves 4

Rinse the fish under cold running water, pat dry with kitchen paper and remove any pin bones with a pair of tweezers.

Boil the cream in a pan and add the frozen petits pois. Season with salt and pepper and then blend until smooth; set aside for later use.

Heat the chicken stock in a pan. Melt a little butter in a pan and sweat the onion until soft, but not coloured. Add the rice and cook for a few minutes, stirring continuously. When the rice is shiny, pour on the wine and cook, still stirring, until fully absorbed. Start adding the hot stock, a ladleful at a time, and reduce the heat to a simmer. Continue adding the hot stock, a little at a time, stirring occasionally, until all the stock is absorbed. The risotto should be rich and creamy, yet the grains of rice should still have a slight bite. To finish the risotto, stir in the fresh peas, grated Parmesan and a tablespoon of butter, then add the pea purée and season with salt and pepper.

Preheat the grill. Warm the tomato halves with a little olive oil, balsamic vinegar and the tarragon leaves. Season the fish, brush with olive oil and cook under the hot grill until cooked and the skin has bubbled.

Serve the risotto on warm plates with the tomatoes around the outside. Place the mullet on top of the risotto and serve immediately.

Braised Trout in Riesling

4 trout, about 200–240g each
60g butter
2 shallots, finely chopped
6 button mushrooms, sliced

250ml Riesling wine
salt and pepper
200ml double cream
squeeze of lemon juice

Serves 4

This is a really simple recipe that lets the food and wine do the talking. Serve with freshly cooked boiled potatoes and peas, accompanied by a glass of Riesling. If you want to experiment with another wine, try a 'flinty' Sauvignon, such as a Reuilly or Pouilly Fumé.

Preheat the oven to 200°C/Gas 6. Prepare the trout by snipping off the fins and removing the gills and eyes. Rinse well under cold running water and pat dry with kitchen paper.

Smear a shallow ovenproof dish that can be used on top of the stove with a little butter. Sprinkle the shallots and mushrooms into the dish and lay the trout on top. Pour in the wine and season. Cover with buttered foil, bring to a simmer then place in the oven for 8–10 minutes.

Remove the trout and pass the cooking liquid through a fine sieve into a pan. Bring to the boil and reduce by half. Add the cream and reduce again until it is a sauce consistency. Finish by whisking in the remaining butter, cut into small dice, check the seasoning and add a squeeze of lemon juice.

To serve, remove the skin from the trout and spoon over the sauce. Accompany with boiled potatoes and peas.

Sea Bass with Fennel and Mushrooms

1 sea bass, about 1kg
1 onion, finely chopped
50g butter
2 large fennel bulbs, finely
  chopped

salt and pepper
250ml double cream
120g button mushrooms,
  finely chopped
1 measure Pernod (optional)

Serves 4

This is a real treat and a favourite of the Roux family. My father loves it with a rich hollandaise with the addition of whipped double cream (mousseline sauce), but my preferred way to eat this fish is with a squeeze of lemon and a glass of good white wine.

Trim, scale and de-bone the sea bass, cutting along the back of the fish and taking care not to pierce any of the skin or flesh. Remove the guts from the back cavity and any remaining pin bones. Rinse the fish under cold running water and dry very thoroughly inside and out. Wrap the fish in a clean cloth and keep refrigerated until required.

In a pan, sweat the onion in the butter for 10 minutes. Do not allow the onion to colour. Add the fennel, then season and cook for 20 minutes until the fennel is soft.

Increase the heat slightly and add the cream. Allow this to reduce by half, then check the seasoning. Add the mushrooms and mix them in. Cook for a further 5 minutes. Add the Pernod, if desired, then spread the mixture on a tray, cover with a piece of buttered greaseproof paper and leave it to cool completely.

Preheat the oven to 200°C/Gas 6. Brush a large sheet of greaseproof paper with oil on one side. Lightly season the inside of the fish with salt and place it on the oiled paper, belly-side down.

Carefully fill the belly cavity of the fish with the fennel and mushroom mixture, and place the fish on its side. Wrap it tightly into a parcel, twisting the ends of the paper.

Cook the fish on a baking tray in the oven for about 20 minutes, turning it after 10 minutes. The fish may be opened at the table or in the kitchen, where the skin may be removed on one side. Wild rice is a good accompaniment.

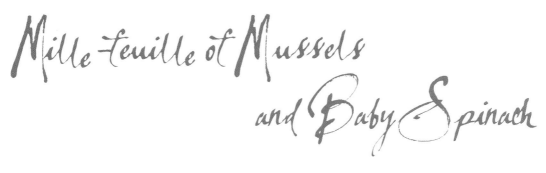

Mille-feuille of Mussels and Baby Spinach

200g puff pastry
5 litres live mussels
500ml dry white wine
1 onion, finely chopped
2 teaspoons Madras curry
   powder

1 small bouquet garni
3 tablespoons butter
120ml double cream
salt and pepper
400g baby spinach leaves

Serves 4

Roll out the puff pastry on a lightly floured surface to a thickness of 2mm. Cut in half, cover and leave to rest in the refrigerator for 20 minutes.

Preheat the oven to 180°C/Gas 4. Put the pastry on a baking sheet and prick with a fork, then put another baking sheet on top and bake for 15 minutes. Remove the top sheet and bake for a further 5 minutes until brown and crisp. Leave to cool, then cut into 12 rectangles, about 6cm x 4cm.

Wash and scrub the mussels in plenty of cold water, discarding any that are open or broken. Put them in a hot pan with the wine, cover and cook over high heat, shaking the pan from time to time. When all the mussels have opened, about 6–8 minutes, drain in a colander set over a bowl to collect the cooking liquid. Pick the mussels and set aside, discarding any that have not opened.

Sweat the onion, curry powder and bouquet garni in the butter until tender. Add the mussel cooking liquid, bring to the boil and reduce by a third. Add the cream and continue to reduce to a light sauce consistency. Reheat the mussels in this sauce without boiling. Remove the bouquet garni and check the seasoning.

Lightly cook the spinach with a drop of olive oil in a wide frying pan until just wilted. Season with salt and pepper.

To assemble, build the 'mille-feuille' on four warm plates, with the spinach, mussels and sauce in between the three layers of puff pastry.

Fried Pollack

2 pollack fillets, about 320g each
flour seasoned with salt for
  dusting
pepper

1 tablespoon vegetable oil
butter
juice of 1 lemon

Serves 4

It's best to cook fish simply, as in this dish, and in my view, pollack is as good as cod when it's fresh and cooked properly. When on holiday in Ireland we never tired of eating this beautiful, flaky, firm-textured fish.

Cut the fillets into portions of about 160g each, with the skin on. Dust the portions in the seasoned flour and place in a hot frying pan with a little smoking vegetable oil. Lower the heat and continue to cook until the fish is golden on both sides, then add a generous spoonful of butter to finish cooking the fish.

Once the butter has turned to a nutty, brown colour, take the pan off the heat and remove the cooked fish. Add a good squeeze of lemon to the juices in the pan, stir and spoon over the fish. Serve at once.

Sole Poached with Saffron and Coriander

2 Dover soles, 1kg each
salt and pepper
1 bunch coriander,
   leaves only, finely chopped
2 tablespoons butter

2 shallots, chopped
275ml dry white wine
generous pinch of saffron
   strands
150ml double cream

Serves 4

Preheat the oven to 180°C/Gas 4. Skin and fillet the soles, lightly score the skin side with a sharp knife, then gently flatten with a cleaver, just enough to break the fibres and give an even thickness. Season the skin side and sprinkle with the chopped coriander. Roll up the fillets, skin side out, and secure each one with a wooden cocktail stick.

Butter an ovenproof dish, add the chopped shallots, wine and fish, and bring to a gentle simmer. Cover with greaseproof paper and place in the oven. After 3–4 minutes, turn the roulades and cook for a further 4 minutes.

Remove from the oven and drain the cooking liquid into a hot saucepan. Add the saffron and reduce by two-thirds. Add the cream and reduce to a fairly rich sauce consistency.

Remove the cocktail sticks and cut each fillet in half. Serve on a bed of peeled red peppers, cut into strips and pan-fried in olive oil.

Sole in a Creamy Carrot Velouté Sauce

4 small Dover soles, 450g each
6 large carrots
1 tablespoon butter
2 shallots, finely chopped
75ml dry white wine

75ml dry white vermouth or
  Noilly Prat
salt and pepper
200g crème fraîche
juice of 1 lemon

Serves 4

Preheat the oven to 180°C/Gas 4. Skin the soles and use a pair of heavy-duty scissors to cut off the head, tail and small bones around the edge of the fish.

Peel the carrots and julienne five of them; set aside. Chop the trimmings and cut the remaining carrot into small dice. Cook in a pan of boiling salted water until well done. Drain and press through a fine sieve.

Lightly butter an ovenproof dish large enough to take the soles; sprinkle the fish with the chopped shallots and carrot juliennes. Pour on the wine and vermouth and bring to the boil in the oven. Season with salt and pepper, cover with buttered greaseproof paper and bake in the oven for 6 minutes, then turn over and cook for a further 6 minutes.

Put the soles on warm plates or a serving dish with twirls of the julienne carrots. Keep warm.

Pour the cooking liquid into a saucepan and bring to the boil. Add the crème fraîche and lemon juice, and check the seasoning. Finally, thicken the sauce with the carrot purée and serve with the sole.

Monkfish Stew with Garlic

1.5kg monkfish
4 tablespoons olive oil
2 onions, thinly sliced
2 fennel bulbs, thinly sliced
2 carrots, thinly sliced
1 leek, white only, sliced
2 bay leaves
salt and pepper
250ml dry white wine
150ml water

Aïoli
10 garlic cloves
2 egg yolks
juice of 1 lemon
250ml olive oil
1 teaspoon Dijon mustard

Serves 6

Known as bourride in French, this monkfish stew is a joy to cook and to eat. Mopping up the broth with big chunks of bread at the end tastes almost too good to be true. You will need 250ml aïoli so if there is any leftover, cover and keep in the refrigerator for a couple of days.

Clean the monkfish, remove the outer membrane and cut into six equal pieces. Leave the pieces on the bone.

Heat a little olive oil in a large pan and sweat the vegetables until tender. Add the bay leaves and a little seasoning. Pour over the wine and water and simmer for about 10 minutes.

Season the monkfish and pan-fry in a non-stick pan over high heat for only 3–4 minutes in total. Remove the fish from the frying pan and add to the vegetables. Cover with a loose-fitting lid and simmer gently for 8–10 minutes. When the monkfish is cooked, remove it with a slotted spoon and set aside. Whisk the aïoli into the vegetable broth. The vegetables should break up and the broth should take on a thick soup consistency. Do not re-boil once the aïoli has been incorporated or it may separate. Serve immediately in deep bowls.

Aïoli

Peel the garlic and remove the central germ from any of the cloves. Place in a mortar or a blender and process, gradually adding all the other ingredients, until you have a smooth paste. Set aside.

Monkfish Cooked with Peppers, Ham and Tomatoes

2 red, 2 green and
  2 yellow peppers
4 ripe plum tomatoes
6 pieces of monkfish,
  about 150g each
6 slices Bayonne or
  Parma ham
olive oil

2 garlic cloves, chopped
1 teaspoon tomato purée
2 sprigs of thyme
1–2 chillies
1 bay leaf
3 tablespoons water
salt and pepper
2 red onions, thinly sliced

Serves 6

Preheat the oven to 220°C/Gas 7. Put the peppers under a hot grill until the skins are burnt and blistered all over. Remove from the heat, cover with clingfilm and leave to cool. When cold, remove the skins, stalks and seeds and cut into long strips.

Blanch the tomatoes in boiling water for 15 seconds, then refresh in ice-cold water. Peel off the skins and cut in half; squeeze out the seeds, then chop roughly.

Wrap each piece of monkfish in a slice of ham, securing the ham with wooden cocktails sticks. Seal over high heat in a roasting pan with a little olive oil, then place in the oven for 7–8 minutes.

Remove the fish from the roasting pan and keep warm. Add the garlic to the pan and cook for 1 minute, then add the tomato purée, thyme, chillies, bay leaf, water and chopped tomatoes and simmer over a low heat for 6 minutes. Season with salt and add any juices that have run out of the fish.

Put a drop of olive oil in a non-stick frying pan and cook the onions until tender and lightly coloured, then add the peppers. Season with salt and pepper and reheat for 1 minute.

Cut each piece of monkfish in half and serve on a spoonful of the tomato sauce. Spoon some of the onion and pepper mixture on top and serve hot.

Grilled Tuna and Crushed White Beans with Pesto

160g dried butter beans
1 litre vegetable stock
60g dry-smoked bacon
  in one piece
2 garlic cloves, peeled

salt and pepper
olive oil
400–500g tuna loin, trimmed
4 tablespoons pesto (page 213)

Serves 4

Soak the butter beans in plenty of water for 8–12 hours.

Drain the beans, then put them in a large pan, cover with the stock and add the smoked bacon and garlic. Bring to the boil, skim, then turn down to a simmer. Cook for 30 minutes, then season lightly and continue to cook until tender, topping up with water if necessary. Take off the heat and leave the beans to cool in their liquid.

Remove the bacon from the beans and chop very finely. Pan-fry in a non-stick pan with a drizzle of olive oil until crispy.

Drain the beans into a bowl, reserving the cooking liquid, and crush them with the back of a fork. Add the bacon and enough of the cooking liquid to make the mixture moist, but not sloppy.

Brush the tuna very lightly with olive oil and season well. Cook on a cast-iron griddle until rare, or to your taste. Using a sharp knife, cut the tuna into slices.

Take the remaining cooking liquid, bring to the boil, add the pesto and froth with a hand-held blender. To serve, rest the slices of tuna on a bed of beans and pour over the sauce.

Fish and Shellfish

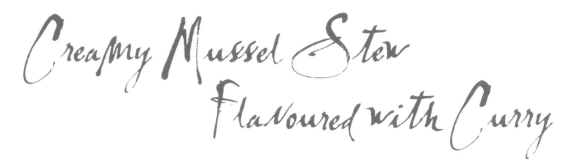

Creamy Mussel Stew Flavoured with Curry

3kg live mussels
olive oil
1 onion, coarsely chopped
3 garlic cloves, crushed
1 sprig thyme and some parsley
stalks

500ml dry white wine
4 shallots, finely chopped
1 tablespoon butter
2 teaspoons mild curry powder
600ml double cream
salt and pepper

Serves 4

Another family favourite, this is often served for lunch at Le Gavroche as a starter, but my father orders a double portion as a main course. If serving as a main course, pilau rice is the perfect accompaniment.

Wash and scrub the mussels in plenty of cold water, discarding any that are open or broken.

Heat a large pan, then add a splash of olive oil and put in the onion, garlic, thyme and parsley stalks. Add the mussels and white wine, cover and leave for 3 minutes. Remove the lid and shake and toss the pan to turn the mussels around. Cover and continue to cook until the mussels have opened.

Pour all the contents into a colander, set over a bowl to collect the juices. Strain the juices though a sieve. Pick the mussels and set aside, discarding any mussels that have not opened.

Sweat the finely chopped shallots in the butter in another pan until they are soft, but not coloured. Add the curry powder and continue to cook for a further 3 minutes, then add the mussel cooking juices. Boil until reduced by half, add the cream and boil again until reduced to sauce consistency. Check the seasoning and fold in the mussels. Serve immediately – do not boil or the mussels will go rubbery.

Turbot spiked with Smoked Salmon and Buttered Cabbage with Sage

225g smoked salmon in 1 piece
6 pieces turbot, 180g each
3 shallots, chopped
olive oil and butter, for cooking
100g fish trimmings and bones
1 tablespoon white wine vinegar
1 bottle Riesling wine

250g butter, cubed
salt and pepper

Buttered cabbage
1 Savoy cabbage
1 carrot, diced
1 sprig sage, shredded
salt and pepper

Serves 6

Cut the smoked salmon into 36 sticks, 2.5cm long and 3mm thick. Using a small pointed knife or darning needle, make six evenly spaced incisions in each piece of turbot and insert the salmon sticks; they should protrude slightly.

Cook the shallots in a little olive oil and butter until deep brown and caramelised. Add the fish trimmings and sweat for 5–6 minutes, stirring frequently. Add the vinegar and wine, then simmer for 20 minutes, skimming frequently. Strain the sauce through a fine sieve into a clean pan, then boil until reduced by two-thirds.

Heat a large non-stick frying pan until very hot. Add a drop of olive oil and cook the turbot until crisp and browned, then turn and cook the other side; this should take no more than 2–3 minutes on each side. Rest on kitchen paper for 3 minutes. To serve, place a bed of buttered cabbage on plates and put the fish on top. Whisk 150g butter, cut into small pieces, into the sauce, season and pour around the fish.

Buttered cabbage

Discard the outer leaves of the cabbage and cut into quarters. Remove the core and shred the leaves finely. Cook in boiling salted water until tender. Refresh in ice-cold water and drain. Sweat the carrot in 50g of butter in a pan for 5 minutes. Add the cabbage and remaining butter, seasoning, shredded sage leaves and enough water to cover. Place over a low heat, cover with greaseproof paper and cook for 10 minutes.

Cockle Risotto with Parsley

1kg fresh cockles, in their shells
300ml dry white wine
200ml chicken stock (page 206)
2 shallots, finely chopped
2 tablespoons unsalted butter
175g arborio rice

50g Parmesan cheese, grated
1 tablespoon mascarpone
salt and pepper
30g flat leaf parsley, coarsely
  chopped

Serves 4

Wash the cockles in several changes of cold water, scrubbing the shells if necessary. Put them in a hot saucepan with 250ml of the wine, cover the pan, and cook over a high heat, shaking the pan from time to time. When all the shells have opened, about 6–8 minutes, drain into a colander set over a bowl to collect the cooking liquid. Remove the cockles from their shells and set aside. Bring the stock to the boil in another pan and set aside.

In a heavy-based pan, sweat the shallots in the butter until translucent but not browned. Add the rice and cook for a few seconds, stirring until the rice is translucent.

Pour in the remaining wine and turn up the heat until the wine has evaporated, stirring constantly. Add a ladleful of the hot cockle cooking liquid and reduce the heat to a simmer. Continue adding the cockle liquid, then the hot stock, a little at a time, stirring occasionally, until all the stock is absorbed and the rice is tender.

Remove from the heat and stir in the cockles, Parmesan and mascarpone. Season to taste, add the parsley and serve immediately, on warm plates.

Crab Quiche

250g plain flour, sifted
120g cold butter, diced
1 teaspoon salt
1 egg
2 tablespoons water
1 tablespoon butter
1 medium leek, split in half
  lengthways and cut into strips
salt and pepper

1 teaspoon Madras
  curry powder
250g fresh white crabmeat
6 egg yolks
2 eggs
200ml milk
400ml double cream
60g grated Gruyère

Serves 8–10

Start by making the shortcrust pastry. Put the flour on a clean, cold surface, make a well in the centre and add the butter, salt and egg. Using your fingertips, work all the ingredients together, gradually drawing in the flour. Once the mixture has a sandy consistency add the water and gently knead the dough until smooth, but do not overwork. Shape into a ball, wrap in clingfilm and leave to rest in the refrigerator for 2 hours.

Preheat the oven to 200°C/Gas 6 and butter a 22cm flan ring. Roll out the dough on a floured surface to a circle about 3mm thick and use this to line the buttered flan ring. Chill for at least 20 minutes. Prick the pastry with a fork, line with greaseproof paper and baking beans and bake in the oven for 20 minutes. Remove the paper and beans and return the pastry shell to the oven for a further 10 minutes or until the base is cooked.

For the filling, melt the butter in a wide pan and gently cook the leek until tender. Season with a little salt, pepper and the curry powder and continue to cook for 2–3 minutes. Put the leeks into a bowl and leave to cool.

Pick the crabmeat to remove any bones or cartilage and add to the leeks. Whisk the egg yolks and eggs, then add the milk and cream. Season and add to the leek and crab. Pour the mixture into the pastry shell and bake in the oven for 15 minutes. Sprinkle the grated cheese over the top and bake for a further 5 minutes or until golden and set. Leave to cool before serving.

Scallops with Five-spice Sauce

500ml strong red wine
1 tablespoon five-spice powder
1 tablespoon caster sugar
1 tablespoon sherry vinegar
300ml veal stock (page 208)

salt
2 tablespoons cold butter
12 fresh, extra-large,
  diver-caught scallops
olive oil

Serves 4

Boil the red wine in a pan until it is reduced by half.

Warm the spice in another pan over a medium heat until it releases a strong aroma, then add the sugar and vinegar. Cook for a further 2–3 minutes, then add the wine and stock. Simmer until the sauce coats the back of a spoon, then pass it through a fine sieve. Season and whisk in the butter to thicken and shine the sauce. It may need a little more sugar, depending on the acidity of the red wine.

Sear the seasoned scallops in a non-stick frying pan with a tiny drizzle of olive oil. The scallops should be caramelised on one side, and slightly undercooked, otherwise they will be chewy.

Arrange the scallops on the plate with a little sauce and serve with fried vegetable crisps or buttered noodles.

Poultry and Game

Roast Bresse Pigeon with Fresh Peas

6 Bresse pigeons, about
  400–450g each
salt and pepper
olive oil
1 large carrot
18 baby onions

400g shelled fresh peas
275g smoked bacon
120g butter, cubed
225ml chicken stock (page 208)
1 round lettuce, shredded

Serves 6

Bresse is a region in France near Lyons, famous for its poultry. The flavour and texture of these birds is quite unique and they command a high price. If you cannot find Bresse pigeons, make sure you choose best-quality young birds.

Preheat the oven to 230°C/Gas 8. Season inside the pigeons with salt and pepper, then smear the pigeons with olive oil and sprinkle them with salt. Place in a hot roasting pan over a high heat on top of the stove and brown the birds all over. Turn them on to their backs and roast in the oven for about 12 minutes; the meat should be rosy pink. Remove the pigeons from the oven, turn them breast side down so the juices permeate the breast meat, cover with foil and leave to rest in a warm place for 15 minutes before serving.

Cut the carrot into 3cm long batons. Cook the onions, carrot batons and peas in a pan of boiling salted water until just tender. Refresh in ice-cold water and drain well. Cut the bacon into thin batons and blanch for 1 minute in a pan of boiling water; drain well.

Melt 1 tablespoon of butter in a wide pan. When it foams, add the bacon and cook until beginning to brown. Add the onions and cook for a further 3 minutes, rolling them around the pan from time to time. Add the peas, carrots and stock and simmer for 10 minutes. Season well, then add the butter a little at a time, shaking the pan so the butter emulsifies and thickens the sauce. Just before serving, fold in the shredded lettuce leaves. Serve with the pigeons.

Chicken and Cashew Nut Curry

2 garlic cloves, roughly chopped
30g piece of fresh ginger, peeled
  and roughly chopped
350ml water
2 green chillies
2 heaped teaspoons turmeric
180g unsalted cashew nuts
3 tablespoons ghee or clarified

butter or vegetable oil
1 teaspoon coriander seeds
1 clove
salt and pepper
1 corn-fed chicken, about 1.6kg
2 medium onions, sliced
125ml plain yogurt
1 bunch coriander, chopped

Serves 4

Put the garlic and ginger in a blender with 125ml water, 1 chilli, turmeric and 80g of the cashew nuts. Heat a drizzle of ghee in a small pan, add the coriander seeds, clove and a little black pepper and fry until they start to pop. Add to the blender and blitz everything together until smooth. Set aside.

Cut the chicken into eight pieces. Heat some of the ghee in a large pan and fry the chicken until golden all over. Remove and drain. Fry the onions in the same pan until lightly coloured. Put the chicken back into the pan, season with salt then pour on the spice mix. Add another 225ml water and bring to a very gentle simmer. Cover with greaseproof paper and continue to cook for 45 minutes, turning and stirring occasionally.

Just before serving pour in the yogurt and simmer for a further 2–3 minutes. Slice the second chilli and gently roast the remaining nuts. Sprinkle the chilli, nuts and chopped coriander over the chicken, check the seasoning and serve immediately.

Chicken Tajine with Olives and Preserved Lemons

1 corn-fed chicken, about 1.8kg
olive oil
2 onions, sliced
salt and pepper
2 garlic cloves, chopped
2 teaspoons turmeric
2 teaspoons paprika
2 teaspoons coriander seeds,
  cracked

300ml chicken stock (page 208)
260g large green olives, pitted
2 preserved lemons, cut into
  wedges
1 bunch coriander leaves,
chopped

Serves 6

With its gutsy flavours, this is a traditional North African dish. Preserved lemons give a slightly bitter sharpness. If you don't have a tajine dish then you can use an ovenproof pot or casserole dish instead.

Cut up the chicken into drumsticks, wings, thighs and breasts. Cut the thighs and breasts in half. Heat a little olive oil in a frying pan and cook the sliced onions over a high heat until soft and caramelised. Put them into a tajine dish.

Preheat the oven to 170°C/Gas 3. Season the chicken pieces, add a little more olive oil to the frying pan and fry the chicken until golden. Turn down the heat and add the chopped garlic, turmeric, paprika and cracked coriander seeds. Cook for a few minutes to bring out the flavours, then add the stock. Bring to the boil and pour into the tajine dish. Sprinkle over the olives and preserved lemons. Cover and cook in the oven for 45 minutes.

Uncover, check the seasoning and drizzle in some more olive oil. Garnish with chopped coriander leaves and serve with bulgur wheat.

Chicken with Walnut Sauce

2 carrots, roughly chopped	2 bay leaves
2 onions, roughly chopped	salt and pepper
3 garlic cloves, roughly chopped	1 good-quality organic chicken
1 leek, roughly chopped	200g walnuts, ground
3 litres water	juice of ½ lemon
1 bunch thyme	nutmeg, grated

Serves 4

Put the carrots, onions, garlic and leek in a deep pan with the water, thyme, bay leaves and salt. If you have the neck, wings and feet of the chicken, add them as well. Bring to the boil and skim, then reduce the heat and simmer for 20 minutes before adding the whole chicken. Cook for 1¼ hours very gently – the stock should tremble or barely simmer. If the chicken is not submerged add a little hot water.

When the chicken is cooked, ladle out 500ml of the cooking liquid and reduce by half over a high heat. Whisk in the powdered walnuts and lemon juice and season with a little pepper and nutmeg.

To serve, carve the chicken into large pieces and ladle on some sauce. Perfect with pasta and braised celery hearts. Keep the rest of the stock for another recipe.

Roast Guinea Fowl with Chickpeas and Olives

120g dried chickpeas
1 bay leaf
1 sprig rosemary
12 garlic cloves, peeled
salt and pepper
1 oven-ready guinea fowl
1 tablespoon crème fraîche

4 tablespoons olive oil,
  plus extra for drizzling
1 tablespoon butter
24 olives, pitted
60ml Madeira
4 anchovies, chopped
1 small bunch basil, roughly
  chopped

serves 4

Soak the chickpeas overnight in cold water.

The next day, rinse the chickpeas and drain. Put in a pan and cover with fresh water. Add the bay leaf and rosemary and bring to the boil. Gently simmer for 45 minutes or until tender – you may have to top up with boiling water. Once the chickpeas are cooked, leave to cool in the water, then drain, reserving 4 tablespoons of the water.

Preheat the oven to 180°C/Gas 4. Put the garlic cloves in a pan and cover with cold water. Add a pinch of salt and bring to the boil. Drain and repeat this three times. This will make the garlic tender, sweet and less aggressive to taste. Set aside.

Season the guinea fowl and add the crème fraîche to the cavity, together with some seasoning. Put the bird in a roasting pan with the olive oil and sear on all sides over a medium heat on top of the stove. Place in the oven and add the butter. Roast for about 40 minutes, basting frequently. When the bird is done, remove from the roasting pan and set aside in a warm place to rest.

Place the roasting pan over a medium-high heat and add the olives, drained chickpeas and garlic. Cook for 4–5 minutes, stirring occasionally. Pour in the Madeira and the reserved cooking water from the chickpeas. Boil for 5 minutes, then add the anchovies, lots of pepper, the juices from the guinea fowl cavity and any more that have run. Just before serving, add the chopped basil and a drizzle of good olive oil.

Chicken Cooked with Beer

1 free-range corn-fed chicken, about 1.5kg
olive oil and butter, for cooking
50g shallots, finely chopped
200g button mushrooms, sliced
1½ tablespoons brandy

1 bottle (33cl) beer, preferably dark ale
1 teaspoon brown sugar
200ml double cream
50g butter
salt and pepper

Serves 4

The original version of this dish was made with cockerel (coq), but these are not readily available commercially, so this recipe has been adapted to use a free-range (preferably organic) chicken.

Preheat the oven to 220°C/Gas 7. Put the chicken on its side in an enamelled, cast-iron pan with a little olive oil and butter and roast for about 40 minutes; baste the bird several times during cooking, turng it on to its other side and finally on to its back, breast upward. When cooked, transfer the chicken to a plate, breast down so that the juices permeate the meat while it rests.

Discard the fat from the roasting pan and add a knob of fresh butter, place over a low heat and sweat the shallots until translucent, stirring with a wooden spoon. Add the mushrooms and cook for a further 3 minutes. Pour in the brandy and scrape the bottom of the pan with the spoon to deglaze fully. When almost dry pour in the beer and sugar and reduce by half. Add the cream and reduce again to a light sauce consistency. Whisk in the butter, cut into small pieces, to give the sauce sheen. Season to taste with salt and pepper. Carve the chicken and add to the hot sauce.

Chicken with Lentils and Thyme

250g Puy lentils
1 carrot
1 onion, cut in half
1 celery stick
1 garlic clove
200g smoked bacon
1 bouquet garni
750ml chicken stock (page 206)
olive oil

12 baby turnips
12 baby new season onions
1 free-range or organic chicken
100g butter
500ml chicken jus (page 208)
12 white mushrooms
3 tablespoons thyme leaves
salt and pepper

Serves 4

This is very simple to make and delicious at any time of year. In summer it is excellent cold, served with a leafy salad dressed with walnut oil. Try to find grelot onions – the type that look like bulbous spring onions.

Soak the lentils in cold water for 1 hour. Drain and put into a wide pan with the carrot, onion, celery, garlic, half the bacon, the bouquet garni and stock. Bring to the boil and simmer for about 30 minutes or until tender (you may need to top up with a little water if necessary). Drain and set aside.

While the lentils are simmering, cut the remaining bacon into large lardons, place in a pan of cold water and bring to the boil for 1 minute. Drain and refresh in cold water, then pat dry. Fry in a hot non-stick pan, adding a little olive oil to prevent sticking, until the lardons begin to crisp.

Peel the turnips and blanch in boiling water for 3–4 minutes. Blanch the baby onions for 2–3 minutes.

Joint the chicken and pan-fry in a little butter until three-quarters cooked.

Bring the chicken jus to the boil in an enamelled cast-iron pot. Add the lentils, turnips, baby onions, mushrooms, and finally the chicken. Simmer for 10 minutes or until the chicken is cooked. Add the remaining butter, cut into small pieces, and add the thyme. Check for seasoning and serve hot.

Chicken Braised in Red Wine

3 small chickens, about
  900g each
1 litre full-bodied red wine
400g piece of smoked bacon
olive oil
1 onion, roughly chopped
1 carrot, roughly chopped
1 celery stick, roughly chopped
1 garlic clove
1 bouquet garni

18 small button mushrooms,
  stalks trimmed and reserved
1 tablespoon plain flour, toasted
  in the oven at 180°C/Gas 4
  until golden brown
300ml port
1.2 litres veal stock (page 208)
salt and pepper
18 button onions
100g butter

Serves 6

Cut each chicken in half lengthways. Cut off the backbone and wing tips to leave six portions consisting of leg and breast. Put these in a stainless steel container, pour on just enough wine to cover, then cover and chill in the refrigerator for 2–3 days.

Preheat the oven to 140°C/Gas 1. Put the bacon in cold water and bring to the boil for 5 minutes; refresh and drain. Cut into lardons 2cm long x 5mm thick, reserving the trimmings.

Drain the chicken and pat dry. Boil the marinade and skim well. Heat the olive oil in a large, heavy-based braising pan and sear the birds well, then remove from the pan. Put the onion, carrot, celery, garlic, bouquet garni, mushroom stalks and bacon trimmings into the pan and cook until caramelised. Add the toasted flour and stir for 3 minutes. Pour in the remaining wine, the port and marinade, and bring to the boil, stirring well until reduced by half. Return the chicken to the pan, add the stock and bring to a simmer. Cover with greaseproof paper and cook in the oven for 1 hour.

Fry the lardons until golden and keep warm. Fry the mushrooms until lightly coloured, season and set aside. Fry the button onions gently until golden; drain and set aside. Remove the chicken, cover and keep warm. Pass the sauce through a sieve into a clean pan; skimming well. Add the button onions and boil for 5 minutes. Add the mushrooms and simmer for 5 minutes. Whisk in the remaining butter and check the seasoning. Pour over the chicken and sprinkle the lardons on top. Serve piping hot.

Caneton Gavroche

1 free-range duck
salt and pepper
olive oil
4 duck or chicken livers
1 tablespoon duck or pork fat

1 shallot, chopped
1 sprig thyme
30g cooked foie gras
brandy

Serves 2

This duck dish dates back to Lower Sloane Street and I think it is exquisite. The secret is to have the liver topping at just the right temperature and consistency. This dish is great served with glazed braised turnips, carrots and a good duck jus.

Preheat the oven to 200°C/Gas 6. Season the duck inside and out and rub salt into the skin. Heat some olive oil in a roasting pan and brown the duck on top of the stove, then place in the oven for about 30 minutes, by which time the breasts should be nicely pink. Remove the legs and continue to roast them until crispy and well done. Remove the duck from the oven and leave to rest. Once the duck has rested, remove the breasts, trim off the skin and keep warm.

Pan-fry the livers over a high heat in the smoking fat, season and add the shallot and thyme, followed by the foie gras. When the livers are rare, deglaze with a little brandy and immediately pour all the contents onto a fine drum sieve, press through using a scraper and keep warm in a saucepan. Reheat and slice the duck breast, then pour over the smooth liver pâté. You may have to beat a little hot stock into the liver to achieve the right texture and fluidity. Serve. The legs can be served afterwards warm, with a little lettuce, watercress and palm heart salad.

Duck Breasts with Shallots, Red Wine and Bone Marrow

2 large duck breasts (magrets)
400g shallots, thinly sliced into
  rounds
2 bottles of red wine
2 litres veal stock (page 206)
salt and pepper

1 bouquet garni
flat leaf parsley
2 pieces of bone marrow,
  soaked in cold water for 2
  hours
100g butter

Serves 4

Preheat the oven to 140°C/Gas 1. Trim most of the fat off the duck breasts, leaving a thin layer of about 3mm, and remove all the sinew from the other side of the breasts. Prick 12 times with a fork.

Put the shallots into a deep-sided, heavy-based pan with the red wine over a medium heat and allow the wine to reduce slowly, until it is one-eighth of its original volume. Add the stock, a pinch of salt and the bouquet garni and cook very slowly, in the oven for about 2½ hours.

Preheat a pan and add the seasoned duck breasts, fatty side down. Enough fat will come out of the magrets in which to cook them. Cook the breasts until they are golden brown on both sides and a nice pink colour inside – 'rose', as we say. This will take about 15 minutes. Remove them from the pan and keep hot.

Having presoaked the marrow in cold water, drain it and cut into 2cm thick slices. Poach the slices gently in simmering salted water, until they are a creamy, white colour, which should take 1–2 minutes. Drain the marrow well on a piece of kitchen paper.

Remove the shallots from the oven and discard the bouquet garni. Check for seasoning and whisk in the butter, cut into little pieces, and the parsley. Carve the duck into long thin slices and arrange the marrow on top. Serve the shallots separately.

Duck Confit and Sauté Potatoes

1 Canard Gras
1kg good-quality coarse sea salt
1 sprig sage
1 sprig thyme

Sauté potatoes
1kg potatoes (Amandine,
  Belle de Fontenay or similar),
  boiled in their skins and cooled
1kg duck or goose fat
salt and pepper
3 garlic cloves
1 bunch of flat leaf parsley,
  chopped

Serves **8**

Canard gras is a duck that has been reared for foie gras. It will weigh about 6kg and may seem expensive but inside it has a whole foie gras. If you cannot find one of these ducks then I suggest eight large duck legs, or two normal ducks.

If using a *canard gras* remove the legs and breasts, trimming off any excess fat. Chop off the head and discard. Remove the skin from the neck and add to the fat, and put the neck with the meat. Take out the foie gras, wrap in clingfilm and refrigerate to use for another recipe. Add the heart and gizzard, cut in half and washed.

Trim all the skin and fat off the carcass. Put all the fat in a pan and cover with water. Bring to a gentle simmer to render. This usually takes about 1 hour – the water should be evaporated and the fat clear. Pour the fat through a fine conical sieve without pressing. Liberally sprinkle the meat with the sea salt and chill for 90 minutes. Wipe off all the salt and moisture with a cloth and put the meat into the warm fat with the sage and thyme. Bring to a very gentle simmer, cover with a greaseproof paper and cook for about 2 hours until tender. Cool in the fat, then chill. It will keep for several weeks.

For the duck confit, preheat the oven to 180°C/Gas 4. Place the meat in a non-stick pan and cook over medium heat until golden. Put into the hot oven for 10–15 minutes.

Sauté potatoes

Peel the potatoes when cool. Cut into 5mm slices and pan-fry in the duck fat. Season and sprinkle with garlic and parsley.

Wild Boar with Chestnuts and Quince

shoulder of boar, about 4kg
1 tablespoon olive oil
salt and pepper
onions, sliced
garlic
bay leaf

quince, peeled and chopped
wine
1 tablespoon quince paste
about 20 chestnuts, cooked and
　peeled

Serves 10–12

My brother-in-law Gérard and his son Julien are keen hunters, and during the game season they regularly shoot wild boar and deer in the mountains of the Cévennes and Ardèche. They make pâtés and terrines with the heads, use the shoulders for stews and the chops for the barbecue. Ribs and belly are salted and air-dried, and sausages are made with special spices.

Preheat the oven to 200°C/Gas 6. Using a boning knife, cut into the two joints of the shoulder. Go in far enough to loosen but not separate them. Place the meat in a large cast-iron dish with a splash of olive oil. Season well with salt and pepper and cook in the oven for 20 minutes.

Add the onions, garlic, bay leaf and quince, and enough wine (rosé is good) to wet the base of the dish. Add the same amount of water, cover with foil and turn the oven down to 150°C/Gas 2 for 1 hour. The meat should be soft and coming off the bone.

Using a slotted spoon, gently take out the meat and place it in a deep serving dish. Cover and keep warm. Put the cooking dish over high heat on top of the stove and add a glass of water (or vegetable stock), the quince paste and chestnuts. Simmer for 5 minutes to melt the quince paste, then pour over the meat and serve.

Rabbit Paella

1 whole rabbit (not wild)
16 slices of smoked bacon, very
thinly sliced
3 green peppers
2 onions, chopped
olive oil
500g paella rice

1 tablespoon tomato purée
2 bay leaves
a pinch of pure saffron
2 teaspoons Espelette chilli
powder
salt and pepper

Serves 8

Who says paella has to be made with bits of chicken and seafood? In inland Spain, rabbit and ham are the traditional ingredients for paella and in my view they are far better. A Spanish rosé wine or even sherry would be a good accompaniment to this dish.

Bone the rabbit, or ask your butcher to do this for you, and cut into bite-sized pieces. Remove the rinds from the bacon and set aside.

Put the rabbit bones in a large pot, cover with water and add the bacon rinds. Bring to the boil and simmer for 25 minutes. Strain the stock and reserve for later – you should have about 800ml.

Preheat the grill. Cook the peppers under the hot grill until their skins have turned black. Cover with clingfilm and leave to cool. When the peppers are cool enough to handle, peel off the skin, remove the seeds and cores and slice into long strips.

Preheat the oven to 180°C/Gas 4. In a large ovenproof pan, sweat the onions in plenty of olive oil for 2–3 minutes. Don't let them colour. Add the peppers and rice and continue to cook for 3–4 minutes, stirring well. Stir in the rabbit, tomato purée, bay leaves, saffron, chilli and seasoning. Pour on the reserved stock and quickly bring to the boil. Lower the heat and lay the slices of bacon over the rice and rabbit. Cover with greaseproof paper and place in the oven for 25 minutes.

Remove from the oven and leave in a warm place for 10 minutes to finish cooking.

Braised Leg of Rabbit with Olives

6 rabbit legs
salt and pepper
4 tablespoons olive oil
1 onion, finely sliced
2 garlic cloves, chopped
1 bay leaf
1 teaspoon tomato purée
100ml dry white wine
6 ripe tomatoes, peeled,
  deseeded and chopped

600ml chicken stock
  (page 208)
12 baby new season onions
6 very thin slices of Parma
  or Bayonne ham
30 black and green olives, pitted
1 tablespoon thyme leaves
1 tablespoon butter

Serves 6

Season the rabbit legs with salt and pepper. Heat a wide heavy-based pan, add half the olive oil and sear the seasoned rabbit legs on all sides over a high heat.

Drain off the fat and replace with a tablespoon of fresh oil, add the onion and lower the heat. Cook until tender, 5–6 minutes, then add the garlic and cook for a further 2 minutes. Add the bay leaf, tomato purée and wine and boil for 1 minute, then add the chopped tomatoes and stock. Cover with greaseproof paper, and simmer for 35–45 minutes until the rabbit is tender. Take off the heat and leave the rabbit in the sauce for at least 20 minutes.

Peel the new season onions, leaving at least 3cm of the green stalk on. Blanch in boiling water, then cut each one into four pieces, and pan-fry in a non-stick pan with a little olive oil to caramelise.

Preheat the grill. Remove the rabbit from the casserole dish, cover and keep warm. Lay the ham on an oiled baking sheet and cook under the hot grill until crisp.

While the ham is grilling, press the sauce through a coarse sieve into a clean pan, add the caramelised onions, olives, thyme and a couple of knobs of butter and bring back to the boil. Place a slice of ham on each rabbit leg, spoon the sauce around and serve. This dish is great served with gnocchi.

Roast Saddle of Hare with Red Wine and Mustard Velouté

2 hare saddles, about 800g each,
  trimmed of all sinews
2 tablespoons olive oil
2 garlic cloves, chopped
2 teaspoons soft brown sugar
100g butter
5 juniper berries, crushed
1 bay leaf
1 sprig thyme
1 onion, sliced

300ml strong dark red wine
  (Syrah or Shiraz)
200ml veal stock (page 208)
salt and pepper
2 tablespoons brandy
2 tablespoons crème de cassis
2 tablespoons port
150ml double cream
1 tablespoon Dijon mustard

Serves 4

Ask your butcher to trim the hare and remove the sinews, but be sure to take these with the meat. Put the sinews and trimmings in a wide pan with the olive oil, garlic and sugar, and caramelise over a high heat. When the meat starts to colour, turn the heat down a little and add a tablespoon of butter – keep the butter frothing. Add the juniper, bay, thyme and onion. When the onion has browned, drain off the fat and pour in the wine. Bring to a simmer, skim and reduce until sticky and almost dry. Add the stock and reduce by half. Pass through a fine sieve, pressing well. Set aside.

Preheat the oven to 200°C/Gas 6. Season the saddles and sear in a roasting tray in olive oil and most of the remaining butter (reserve 1 tablespoon) until evenly coloured. Roast for 12 minutes, basting occasionally. Remove from the oven and leave to rest for 15 minutes in a warm place before carving.

Drain the fat from the tray and pour in the alcohol. Bring to the boil, then pass through a fine sieve into the first sauce made with the trimmings. To finish the sauce, bring to the boil, add the cream and simmer for 5–6 minutes. Whisk in the remaining butter and the mustard, and check the seasoning. Serve with the hare.

Peppered Haunch of Venison

1 haunch of venison, about
  1.6kg, skinned and trimmed
2 tablespoons cracked white
  and black peppercorns
salt
2–3 tablespoons olive oil
200g cold butter
3 shallots
2 celery sticks
1 carrot

1 sprig thyme
1 bay leaf
brandy
300ml dark strong red wine
1 tablespoon jelly
4 tablespoons red wine vinegar
500ml veal stock (page 208)
1 tablespoon crushed green
  peppercorns

Serves **8**

Ask your supplier for venison that has been hung for 10–14 days in its skin. Once it has been trimmed and skinned, rub with the cracked black and white peppercorns, salt and a little olive oil. Set aside for 20 minutes, so the mixture can permeate before the meat is cooked.

Preheat the oven to 200°C/Gas 6. In a hot roasting pan, heat the olive oil and half the butter and evenly colour the haunch on each side. Add the vegetables, thyme and bay leaf, then place in the oven and roast for 35–40 minutes, basting occasionally and turning once. To check whether the meat is done, push a barding needle into the centre for a few seconds and remove. It should be lukewarm for pink meat. Leave the meat in a warm place to rest for 20–30 minutes before slicing.

Drain all the fat out of the pan but keep the vegetables. Over a high heat, add a little brandy to deglaze the pan, then add the wine, jelly and vinegar. Boil, scraping the bottom of the tray well to lift off the roasting sugars, until it is reduced by two-thirds. Add the stock and reduce again by half. Pass through a fine sieve and add any juices that have run from the venison. Whisk in the remaining cold butter and crushed green peppercorns. Serve with the venison.

Haunch of Venison with Lemon and Honey

leg of venison, about 3kg
1 tablespoon olive oil
salt and pepper
juice of 1 lemon
4 tablespoons clear honey

4 onions, roughly sliced
1 large or 2 small lemons, cut
  into wedges
1 sprig thyme
1 good glass of white wine

Serves 8

Rub the venison leg with a little olive oil, salt, pepper, lemon juice and 1 tablespoon of honey. Cover with clingfilm and leave to marinate overnight.

Preheat the oven to 220°C/Gas 7. Heat a roasting tray on top of the stove, add a good splash of olive oil and sear the venison until it is coloured on all sides, then place it in the oven for 10 minutes.

Remove the venison from the oven and add the onions, lemons, the remaining honey, the thyme and wine.

Turn the oven down to 180°C/Gas 4 and put the meat back in the oven for about 30 minutes. Turn the heat off and leave the venison in the oven for a further 30 minutes. Remove and take to the table to carve.

Hot Venison Pies

1kg venison meat, trimmed
300g fatty pork meat
300g veal
800g pork fat
salt and pepper
2 tablespoons brandy
2kg puff pastry
1 egg, beaten

Farce à gratin
150g venison liver
100g raw foie gras
1 tablespoon duck fat
2 shallots, chopped
1 sprig thyme
1 bay leaf
2 tablespoons brandy

Serves 20

First make the *farce à gratin* – if you can't find venison liver you can use chicken livers. Sear the liver and raw foie gras in a very hot frying pan with the duck fat. After a few seconds, add the chopped shallots, thyme and bay leaf, then season well. When the livers are still very pink, add half the brandy and take off the heat. Press all of this, including the liquid, through a coarse drum sieve and set aside.

Cut all the other meats and fat into small chunks, season with salt and pepper, then cover and chill in the refrigerator overnight.

The next day, mince using a hand mincer with a 5mm size disc. It is best to refrigerate the mincer before using to keep everything as cold as possible. Once this is done, add the *farce à gratin*, seasoning and remaining brandy. Shape the mixture into small balls weighing about 120g.

Preheat the oven to 180°C/Gas 4. Butter rings, about 8cm across, and line with the rolled out pastry. Put a ball of meat mixture in each one and top with discs of pastry. Make a hole in the top of each pie and insert a roll of greaseproof paper as a chimney to let the steam out during cooking. Brush with beaten egg and bake in the oven for 20 minutes.

Meat

Roast Leg of Lamb with Rosemary and Garlic

24 small new potatoes, peeled
salt and pepper
1 leg of lamb, about 1.8–2kg
3 tablespoons olive oil
2 heads garlic

2 sprigs rosemary
butter
24 pearl onions, peeled
200ml dry white wine
200ml water

Serves 6–8

Preheat the oven to 200°C/Gas 6. Parboil the new potatoes in a pan of salted water for 3 minutes. Drain and set aside.

Rub the leg of lamb with a little olive oil, salt and pepper. Peel 3 garlic cloves and cut in half lengthways. Make six incisions in the leg of lamb and insert a piece of garlic and a small piece of rosemary into each one. Break up the rest of the garlic without peeling. Place the lamb in a hot roasting pan with the rest of the olive oil and sear over a medium heat until golden on all sides. Add 2 tablespoons butter and continue to heat until foaming. Put the parboiled potatoes, pearl onions and the rest of the garlic and rosemary into the foaming butter around the lamb. Season and roast in the oven for 10 minutes. Turn the potatoes and onions occasionally and baste the lamb with the fat. Turn the oven down to 190°C/Gas 5 and continue to roast for 45–60 minutes.

Take the meat and vegetables out of the pan and keep warm. Pour out most of the fat and add the wine, followed by the water. Bring to the boil and scrape the pan with a spatula to lift the roasting sugars. Continue to boil and add any juices that have run from the leg of lamb. When reduced by half, whisk in a knob of butter, then pass the sauce through a fine sieve. Serve with the lamb and vegetables.

Braised Shoulder of Spring Lamb

2 shoulders of baby lamb
olive oil
24 button onions, peeled
sea salt
3 garlic cloves, chopped
1 teaspoon cumin seeds
1 chilli, cut in half lengthways
  and deseeded

3 plum tomatoes, peeled,
  deseeded and chopped
100ml Madeira
generous pinch of saffron
  strands
200ml fresh orange juice
500ml chicken stock (page 206)

Serves 6

Preheat the oven to 190°C/Gas 5. Take an ovenproof casserole dish with plenty of room to hold the shoulders laid flat, put over a high heat and add a generous amount of olive oil. Brown the lamb well on both sides.

Lower the heat to medium and add the button onions and a little salt. Shake the pan from time to time so that the onions start to get a good colour. After about 5 minutes add the garlic, cumin seeds, chilli and tomatoes, stir well and increase the heat to high. Pour in the Madeira and add the saffron, and when it comes to the boil add the orange juice and stock. Bring back to the boil, then partially cover the pan and cook in the oven for 1 hour, stirring and turning the meat occasionally.

Leave to cool completely, then remove the lamb from the casserole and chill in the refrigerator for 1 hour.

Using a heavy knife or cleaver, cut the shoulders into three portions at the joints.

To serve, reheat the meat in a non-stick frying pan with a little olive oil until caramelised. Remove the chilli from the sauce, then reheat the sauce until piping hot. Pour the sauce over the meat and serve with couscous.

Stuffed Saddle of Lamb with Spinach and Garlic, Saffron Jus

1 saddle of lamb (with kidneys)
200g caul fat
salt and pepper
20 garlic cloves, peeled
100g butter
olive oil
900g spinach

100ml double cream
2 egg yolks
1 large onion, chopped
125ml sweet white wine
2 pinches of saffron strands
500ml chicken stock (page 206)

Serves 6–8

Remove the skin and excess fat from the lamb. Bone the saddle from the belly, removing the fillets but without making any holes on the upper side. Cut the flaps to 12cm on each side, lay the lamb on the stretched caul fat and season. Chop the bones.

Preheat the oven to 200°C/Gas 6. Blanch the garlic in a pan of boiling salted water for 1 minute, then drain. Put the garlic on a sheet of foil with a tablespoon of butter and a little oil, season, then fold over and seal the foil. Cook in the oven for 20 minutes. Boil the cream until reduced by half and blanch the spinach in a pan of boiling salted water. Refresh in cold water, squeeze dry and chop roughly. Cut the lamb kidneys into small dice, toss in a hot pan for 15 seconds, then drain and add to the spinach, with the cream, egg yolks and roasted garlic. Turn the oven up to 220°C/Gas 7.

Spoon some of the spinach mixture down the centre of the boned lamb saddle, place the fillets on top and cover with the remaining spinach. Roll the belly flaps over the centre, wrap in the caul fat and tie with string. Roast in the oven for 30 minutes, then remove from the oven and leave to rest in a warm place for at least 30 minutes. Meanwhile, drain the fat from the roasting pan and add the bones and onion with a little olive oil. Cook over medium heat, stirring frequently. When browned, deglaze with the wine, and allow to reduce by half. Add the saffron and stock and reduce by two-thirds, skimming off the fat. Strain into a clean pan and whisk in a little butter to thicken and shine the sauce. Serve immediately with the lamb.

Lamb Tajine

1 boned lamb shoulder
2 tablespoons olive oil
2 garlic cloves, chopped
3 onions, chopped
2 teaspoons turmeric
2 teaspoons coriander seeds, crushed

2 teaspoons cumin seeds
1 lemon, cut into 8 wedges
1 tablespoon honey
300ml chicken or vegetable stock (page 208)
50g whole blanched almonds, toasted

Serves 4–6

Preheat the oven to 140°C/Gas 1. Cut the lamb into 3cm chunks. Heat the olive oil in a cast-iron casserole dish and pan-fry the lamb until golden. Add the garlic, onions and spices to the dish and continue to cook and stir over a medium heat for about 10–15 minutes.

Add the lemon, honey and stock to the dish and bring to a simmer. Cover and cook in the oven for 1 hour.

Stir in the toasted almonds and serve in traditional tajine dishes if you have them.

Leg of Lamb Cooked for Seven Hours

Marinade
½ bottle full-bodied red wine
2 garlic cloves, crushed
1 small onion, thickly sliced
1 carrot, thickly sliced
1 sprig thyme
1 sprig rosemary
2 tablespoons virgin olive oil
2 cloves
1 tablespoon white peppercorns
3 tablespoons brandy
2 tablespoons red wine vinegar

1 leg of lamb, about 3kg
200g pork back fat
100g butter
2 tablespoons olive oil
150g smoked bacon
2 bottles full-bodied red wine
½ bottle port
salt and pepper
3 litres veal stock (page 208)

Serves 8

Trim the leg of lamb by removing the aitch bone and scoring the skin. Cut 12cm long strips of pork back fat (5mm) and use to bard the leg of lamb lengthways at least six times. For the marinade mix all of the ingredients together, cover lamb, and chill. Turn the meat several times a day so it absorbs the flavours. Marinate for at least a week.

Preheat the oven to 140°C/Gas 1. Drain the lamb, reserving the vegetables and the marinade. Heat the butter and olive oil in a braising pan and cook the lamb over a medium-high heat until golden brown. Remove the lamb and if the fat is burnt, discard it and use fresh butter to cook the vegetables (including the marinated vegetables) until golden. Add the bacon, then deglaze the pan with the wine, port and marinade. Put over a high heat and reduce by two-thirds, then add the lamb, season and cover with stock. Bring to the boil and skim. Check the seasoning. Cover and cook in the oven for 7 hours! Keep an eye on it: you may have to top up with liquid. The meat should be tender and nearly falling off the bone.

Leave to cool in the sauce. When cold, carefully remove the lamb and strain the sauce through a fine sieve. Check for seasoning and consistency; reduce the sauce if necessary. Pour the sauce over the meat and chill overnight.

Reheat, basting the meat occasionally. Bring to the table and serve with a spoon.

Lamb Cutlets
with Tarragon Vinegar

60g clarified butter
12 lamb cutlets, about 800g
 in total
30g butter
2 medium shallots, finely
 chopped

100ml dry white wine
1 tablespoon tarragon vinegar
400ml double cream
2 tablespoons chopped tarragon
salt and pepper

Serves 4

Heat the clarified butter in a pan, add the lamb cutlets with a little fresh butter, too, and brown them on all sides. When the cutlets are cooked to your liking, take them out and keep warm.

Pour off the excess fat from the pan and add the rest of the fresh butter. Add the shallots and sweat them gently for a few minutes. Deglaze with the white wine, reduce a little, then add the vinegar. Reduce this by half, and then add the cream and chopped tarragon. Reduce by half again and check the seasoning.

Arrange the lamb cutlets on serving plates, coat the cutlets lightly with the sauce and serve with little roast potatoes, carrots and French beans.

Roast Rib of Beef with Cep Gratin

1 rib of beef, 500–600g
  with the bone
olive oil
salt and pepper

Cep gratin
220g fresh ceps (porcini
mushrooms), thinly sliced
3 tablespoons olive oil

3 shallots, chopped
1 tablespoon butter
2 slices of Parma ham, diced
1 spring onion, chopped
½ garlic clove, chopped
2 tablespoons chopped
  flat leaf parsley
2 tablespoons dry white
  breadcrumbs

Serves 2

I like my beef hung for 21 days on the bone; most butchers hang meat for 7–14 days, but the extra week ensures tenderness and gives it the depth of flavour that a rib should have. Fore rib has a vein of fat running through it that melts as it cooks to keep the meat beautifully moist and full of flavour.

Preheat the oven to 220°C/Gas 7. Heat a roasting pan over a high heat and seal the beef all over in a little olive oil, then place in the oven and roast for 8 minutes: the meat should be rare. Take out of the oven and leave to rest for 10 minutes before serving. Carve at the table and fight over who has the bone!

Serve the beef with Béarnaise sauce (page 212) and cep gratin.

Cep gratin

Preheat the oven to 200°C/Gas 6. Pan-fry the ceps in the olive oil until golden brown, then season and drain in a colander.

Sweat the shallots in the butter, then add the ham. When the shallots are soft add the spring onion and garlic and cook for a further 2 minutes, stirring occasionally.

Mix the ceps and parsley with the shallots. Place in a gratin dish, sprinkle the breadcrumbs over the top and bake in the hot oven for 10 minutes.

Grilled Rib of Beef

2 ribs of beef
(about 350g each)

olive oil
salt and pepper

Serves 4

There is no secret to a good rib of beef: to me it's obvious that if you buy beef from a small farm (not necessarily organic, although most are) that takes care of its animals and feeds and breeds them properly, you have a good chance of enjoying a fine piece of meat. The meat should be well hung – four weeks in my view.

Rub the trimmed ribs with a little olive oil, salt and pepper. Set the meat on the grill over a medium heat. This is a thick cut of meat so it needs to cook slowly. Turn so that it cooks and marks evenly. The beef should take 20 minutes for medium rare.

Don't forget to let it rest at least 10 minutes in a warm place before carving.

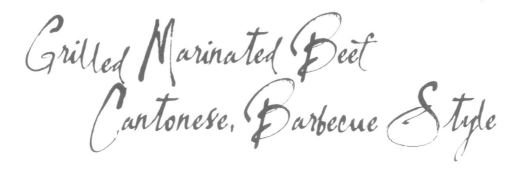

Grilled Marinated Beef Cantonese, Barbecue Style

500g beef sirloin (trimmed
  weight), no fat or sinew
2 tablespoons tomato ketchup
1 tablespoon clear honey
1 tablespoon dark soy sauce
4cm piece of fresh ginger,
  peeled and finely chopped

2 garlic cloves, peeled
½ tablespoon coarsely ground
black or white pepper
1 tablespoon Worcestershire
  sauce
1 tablespoon sesame oil

Serves 4

This is delicious cooked on the barbecue or simply pan-fried in a non-stick pan without any fat. It can even be cooked under a hot grill. I use this recipe for little canapés served at Le Gavroche before a meal. As a main course, serve with stir-fried or grilled vegetables, or freshly cooked rice.

Slice the beef against the grain into thin 3mm slices and place in a non-metallic shallow dish.

Mix all the remaining ingredients together to make a marinade. Cover the beef with the mixture, then cover and leave to marinate for at least 2 hours, but no more than 12.

Remove the meat from the marinade. Cook over a high heat on a barbecue or in a non-stick pan to caramelise, and serve immediately.

Spicy Raw Beef with Quail's Eggs

800g sirloin steak, 400g for starter	2 tablespoons chopped parsley
12 cornichons (small French gherkins), chopped	dash of brandy
6 shallots, finely chopped	Worcestershire and Tabasco sauce, to taste
1 tablespoon super-fine capers	4 quail's eggs
1 tablespoon tomato ketchup	salt
1 tablespoon Dijon mustard	80–100g cooked truffle, thinly sliced
2 tablespoons mayonnaise	sour cream

Serves 4

Use sirloin steak, as the grain of the meat is not as stringy as fillet and not as chewy as topside. The beef should be of the best quality, never frozen, and matured for only a week. All the ingredients can be prepared in advance; even the meat can be chopped a few hours before serving as long as it is kept cold, but the mixing must be done at the last minute.

Remove any sinew and fat from the sirloin, then with a sharp, thin-bladed knife cut into thin slices. Lay these flat on a chopping board and cut into strips, then cut across to make very small dice. You can use an electric mincer, but I find it changes the texture of the meat. Put the chopped steak into a big bowl in the refrigerator.

Just before serving, mix the cornichons, shallots, capers, ketchup, mustard, mayonnaise, parsley and brandy with the chopped meat. Season with Worcestershire and Tabasco sauce and salt to taste, then divide the meat into four portions and shape into patties.

I like to place some thinly sliced truffle and a soft-boiled quail's egg on top and serve with a curly endive salad and French fries. Drizzle the plate with sour cream thinned down with a little cold water.

Roast Rib of Veal Glazed with a Herb Crust

6 ribs of veal, trimmed,
  250g each with the bone
salt and pepper
4 tablespoons olive oil

Herb and pepper crust
25g each of basil, chives, parsley,
  rosemary, tarragon and thyme

25g black and white
  peppercorns
250g butter, softened
100g beef bone marrow or
  butter
375g dry white breadcrumbs
150g Gruyère cheese, grated
80g Cheddar cheese, grated

Serves 6

Preheat the oven to 200°C/Gas 6. Season the veal with salt and pepper and place in a heated roasting pan with the olive oil. Seal well on both sides, then place in the oven for 12 minutes – turn after 6 minutes – for pink-cooked meat. Cover with foil and leave to rest in a warm place for 10–15 minutes before serving.

Preheat the grill. Cut 5mm thick slices of the herb crust and roll it out between two sheets of clingfilm, to the size of the chops – you may have to cut and reshape the crust as the chops are rarely perfect rounds. Put the shaped crust on the chops, then place the chops under the hot grill until the crust bubbles and starts to turn crisp and brown. Serve immediately. You can serve the veal with a tomato and olive sauce and confit potatoes.

Herb and pepper crust

Wash and dry the herbs, then roughly chop. Crush the peppercorns. Put the herbs, peppercorns, butter and all the remaining ingredients into a blender and blend until smooth. Form the mixture into a large sausage shape, wrap in clingfilm and tie both ends. Freeze until ready to use.

Veal Stew with White Wine Sauce

1kg breast of veal,
  cut into 4 cm chunks
1 large onion, peeled and
  studded with 2 cloves
2 carrots, peeled
1 leek, white part only
1 bouquet garni

salt and pepper
24 small cocktail onions, peeled
250g small button mushrooms
300ml double cream
2 egg yolks whisked with 2
  tablespoons crème fraîche

Serves 6–8

Put the veal in a pan, cover generously with cold water and bring to the boil. Turn down to a gentle simmer and skim off any froth. After 30 minutes add the vegetables, bouquet garni and a little salt. Continue to simmer for a further 80 minutes, topping up with boiling water if necessary.

While this meat is simmering, carefully decant about ½ litre of the cooking liquid and pour over the small cocktail onions in a separate pan. Simmer until tender, then add the mushrooms. Cover and simmer for a further 10 minutes until cooked. Now drain and pour the liquid back into the meat pot. Keep the onions and mushrooms warm. When the meat is tender, gently drain off and put in a tureen, discarding the vegetables and bouquet garni. Cover and keep warm.

Bring the cooking liquid to a rapid boil for 15 minutes or until reduced by half. Add the double cream, boil again for 5 minutes, then take the pan off the heat and stir in the whisked egg yolk mixture. Check for seasoning, pour though a fine sieve over the meat and garnish with the cocktail onions and mushrooms.

Roast Rib of Veal with Pasta

800–900g trimmed rib of veal,
   remove the backbone and
   French trim; tie with butcher's
   string
salt and pepper
4 tablespoons vegetable oil
2 tablespoons butter
1 onion, chopped
1 carrot, chopped
1 celery stick, chopped

1 garlic clove, chopped
300ml water

Creamed pasta
160g pasta
8 button mushrooms, finely
   chopped
180ml double cream
1 tablespoon crème fraîche
80g Emmental cheese, grated

Serves 4

Preheat the oven to 180°C/Gas 4. Rub the veal with salt and pepper. In a roasting pan just the right size for the veal, preferably a cocotte (cast-iron cooking pot), heat the vegetable oil until it's hot enough to sear the veal on all sides. Add the butter and chopped vegetables and garlic and cook in the oven for 30 minutes, turning twice.

Remove the veal, cover lightly and leave to rest in a warm place. Remove the vegetables and set aside. Drain off as much fat as possible and return the pan to a hot stove, stirring and scraping the bottom for 2–3 minutes. Pour on the water and continue to stir and reduce for 3–4 minutes. Add in the juices that have run off the veal and press through a fine sieve. Serve this sauce with the veal, roasted vegetables and creamed pasta.

Creamed pasta

Cook the pasta in a pan of boiling salted water until tender. Rinse and drain well, shaking the colander to remove all the water.

Preheat the grill. Put the mushrooms in a pan with the double cream and simmer until the liquid is reduced by half. Gently fold in the pasta, crème fraîche and seasoning. Pour the mixture into an ovenproof dish, sprinkle with the grated cheese and glaze under the hot grill for a few minutes.

Roast Rack of Pork, Charcutière Sauce

1 rack of organic pork
  (8 bones from the neck end)
salt
4 tablespoons olive oil
180g butter
24 new potatoes (preferably
  Charlotte or Vivaldi), peeled
24 garlic cloves, peeled
4 sprigs thyme
2 bay leaves
250ml dry white wine

1 tablespoon white wine vinegar
4 shallots, peeled and chopped
300ml veal stock (page 208)
1 tablespoon cracked black and
  white pepper
1 tablespoon Dijon grain
  mustard
8 plum tomatoes, peeled,
  deseeded and diced
4 tablespoons cornichons (small
  French gherkins), thinly sliced

Serves 6–8

Preheat the oven to 190°C/Gas 5. Season the pork and cover the tips of the bones with foil. Place in a hot roasting pan with the olive oil and 100g of the butter and roast in the oven for 30 minutes. After 5 minutes, put the potatoes, garlic cloves, thyme and bay leaves into the roasting pan and season lightly. Make sure the roasting pan is large enough to accommodate all the ingredients without them being squashed.

After 30 minutes, turn the oven down to 150°C/Gas 2 and roast for a further 15 minutes, basting frequently. Remove the pork, cover with foil and leave to rest in a warm place for 45 minutes. The new potatoes and garlic should by now be golden: if not, turn the oven up to 200°C/Gas 6 and put the pan back in the oven for another 5 minutes. Remove the potatoes and garlic and keep warm.

Discard the fat from the roasting pan, pour in the wine and vinegar and bring to the boil, scraping the pan with a spatula to loosen all the caramelised juices. In another pan, sweat the shallots in 25g of butter, then strain the wine on to the shallots, add the stock and cracked pepper and reduce by two-thirds. Whisk in the remaining butter and the mustard, and stir in the diced tomatoes. Finally, just before serving, add the cornichons. Carve the pork into chops and serve with the sauce.

Pork Shoulder Stew with Potatoes and Chorizo Sausage

1.2kg pork shoulder, boned
salt and pepper
3 garlic cloves, peeled
2 onions, sliced

1kg potatoes (preferably Ratte,
  Rosevale, Charlotte), peeled
3 spicy cooking chorizo
  sausages, 60g each, cut in half
600g turnips tops

Serves 6

This recipe for a rustic stew has its origins in the Pyrenées and it's perfect for a cold winter's night. The turnip tops are an important part of the dish, but you can use chard instead if you prefer. A straightforward Rioja from the Tempranillo grape suits this very peasant-style stew.

Be sure to ask your butcher for the bones from the pork so they can be cooked with the meat for added flavour.

Cut the pork into three pieces. Place in a large pan with the bones and cover with cold water. Season and add the garlic and onions. Bring to a simmer, skim well and leave to cook gently for 1½ hours. The pork should be tender by the end of the cooking time. Remove the meat from the pan and slice thickly. Cover and set aside. Discard the bones.

Cut the potatoes into large chunks. Add them to the pan you used for the pork and cook for 25 minutes or until tender. You may need to top up the pan with boiling water occasionally.

Once the potatoes are cooked, add the chorizo, turnip tops and the slices of pork. Season and simmer for a further 5–6 minutes. Serve in big bowls.

Pork Pie with Chestnut and Apple

275g puff pastry
125g cooked ham
250g pork shoulder
200g smoked bacon
2 onions, finely chopped
2 tablespoons olive oil
1 tablespoon butter

2 garlic cloves, chopped
1 sprig of thyme, leaves only
2 apples (preferably Cox or
  Braeburns)
250g whole chestnuts
3 eggs
salt and pepper

Serves 6

This pie comes from the Cévennes, the chestnut-growing area of France. It can be eaten hot, but in my view is far better cold. You can use fresh chestnuts but they do take a long time to peel, so I recommend buying them ready cooked and peeled in vacuum packs, or even dried from health food shops.

Butter a 26cm pie or flan ring. Divide the pastry into two pieces, one slighly larger than the other. Roll out the larger piece and use to line the buttered pie or flan ring. Put in the refrigerator.

Mince the ham, pork and bacon. Sweat the onions in the olive oil and butter until soft and translucent. Add the garlic and thyme leaves and continue to cook for about 4–5 minutes. Leave to cool.

Peel, core and halve the apples, then slice them finely. Fold the slices in the pork mixture with the onions, chestnuts and 2 of the eggs. Season, being generous with the pepper.

Preheat the oven to 200°C/Gas 6. Pack the mixture into the pie base. Beat the remaining egg. Roll out the other piece of pastry and place it on top of the pie, sealing the edges with the beaten egg. Brush the top of the pie with more egg and make a little hole in the top to let out steam. Cook in the oven for 20 minutes, then turn the oven down to 180°C/Gas 4 and cook for a further 25 minutes.

Grilled Neck End Pork Chops, Oriental Style

6 neck-end pork chops,
   rind off, about 150g each
3 garlic cloves, peeled
2 tablespoons fish sauce
   (nam pla)

2 tablespoons oyster sauce
3 tablespoon light soy sauce
1 tablespoon honey
juice of 1 orange
coarsely ground pepper

Serves 6

I find neck-end chops tastier than loin chops because they have some fat running through them. These chops are particularly tasty when grilled, and perfect when cooked on the barbecue. If you would like to serve some wine with these chops, either a white wine like Pinot Grigio or a red wine such as Pinotage go well with this dish.

Put the chops in a shallow non-metallic dish.

Purée the garlic, then put into a bowl. Add the fish sauce, oyster and soy sauces, honey, orange juice and plenty of pepper and mix together to make a marinade. Rub this marinade over the chops and chill in the refrigerator for 2 hours.

Preheat the grill and cook the chops under the hot grill, or you can barbecue them if you wish.

Desserts

Lemon Pancake Gâteau

125g unbleached white flour
80g wholemeal flour
500ml milk
pinch of salt
grated zest of 2 lemons
vegetable oil
fresh berries, to serve

Lemon butter
3 eggs
juice and grated zest of 3
 lemons
160g caster sugar
75g butter

Serves **8**

To make the pancakes, mix the eggs into the flours with a whisk, then add the milk gradually to avoid any lumps. Finally, mix in the salt and lemon zest and leave the batter to rest for 1 hour.

Add a smear of vegetable oil to a non-stick pan and cook the pancakes. They should be very thin and well cooked, almost dry.

Preheat the oven to 200°C/Gas 6. Line the base of a round, non-stick cake tin, about the same diameter as the pancakes, with greaseproof paper. Place a pancake in the tin followed by a thin layer of the lemon butter. Repeat the layers until all the pancakes and lemon butter have been used. Cover with greaseproof paper and bake in the oven for 20 minutes. Leave to cool in the tin, then cut into slices when cold and serve with fresh berries. If you like, decorate with mint and orange zest.

Lemon butter

Whisk the eggs, sugar, lemon juice and zest together in a saucepan. Place over a medium heat and stir continuously until the mixture thickens. Do not boil. Pass the mixture through a fine sieve, then whisk in the butter, cut into small pieces. Cover and leave to cool.

Classic Raspberry Tart

125g caster sugar
125ml water
1 tablespoon
  raspberry alcohol
750g large plump
raspberries
icing sugar

Sweet pastry
180g butter
375g flour
90g sugar
2 egg yolks
1 tablespoon
  double cream

Almond cream
100g butter, softened
100g icing sugar
100g ground almonds
2 eggs

Raspberry coulis
300g raspberries
60–80g icing sugar

Serves 8

When raspberries are in season and bursting with sweetness and flavour, there is no other fruit to equal them. This particular tart reminds me of my apprenticeship as a pastry chef.

Make a syrup by mixing the caster sugar with the water. Bring to the boil, then set aside to cool. Add the raspberry alcohol. Preheat the oven to 200°C/Gas 6 and lightly butter a 24cm tart ring. Roll out the sweet pastry dough on a floured surface to 2–3mm thickness and line the buttered tart ring. Spoon in the almond cream until the tart is two-thirds full, then bake in the oven for 20–30 minutes until golden and fully cooked. Brush the tart with the flavoured syrup. Neatly arrange the raspberries on the tart and dust with icing sugar. Serve with cream and raspberry coulis.

Sweet pastry

Mix the butter, flour and sugar together in a bowl. Gradually add the egg yolks and cream until the dough comes together. Do not overwork. Wrap in clingfilm and chill for at least 2 hours.

Almond cream

Beat the butter, add the sugar and ground almonds. Beat until the mixture is pale and creamy. Add the eggs one at a time.

Raspberry coulis

Blitz the raspberries and sugar together. The amount of sugar depends on the ripeness of the fruit, so taste before adding the full amount.

Iced Red Berry Soufflé

1kg mixed berries
   (strawberries, raspberries,
   blueberries, blackcurrants),
   plus extra to decorate
400g caster sugar

juice of 1 lemon
500ml water
4 egg whites
80ml whipping cream

Serves 10

Hull and, if necessary, wash the fruit. Blend with 150g of the sugar, then pass through a fine sieve and add lemon juice to heighten the taste if required. Prepare 10 individual soufflé dishes (9cm diameter x 6cm deep) by tying a piece of greaseproof paper around the edge to form a collar that stands 5cm above the rim.

In a clean pan, pour in the water and add the remaining 250g of sugar, then leave over a low heat until the sugar has dissolved. When the sugar has completely dissolved, bring to the boil, skim off the foam and cook to 120°C on a sugar thermometer. Put the egg whites into the bowl of an electric mixer and beat until foamy. With the whisk still running, pour the hot sugar directly on to the egg whites, avoiding the beaters. Continue beating until the meringue is cool.

Whip the cream until soft peaks form, and fold into the fruit pulp. Delicately fold in the meringue, then spoon into the prepared soufflé dishes. Freeze for 12 hours.

Decorate with fresh berries and, if you like, serve with a sauce made by puréeing 500g berries with 100g caster sugar, sharpening the taste with a little lemon juice.

Salted Caramel Walnut Tart

100ml single cream
200g salted butter
200g liquid glucose
400g caster sugar
100ml water
400g walnuts (shelled weight)

Sweet pastry
450g flour
150g butter
90g sugar
4 egg yolks
2 tablespoons cream

Serves 10

If possible, use fresh walnuts from the Périgord region in October and November. It's worth the extra effort of cracking them open yourself. This tart is delicious served with Amaretto or a tawny port, as port and walnuts are a classic combination.

Roll out the sweet pastry dough on a lightly floured surface and use to line a 22cm x 3cm flan ring. Keep back a third of the dough to make the lattice top.

Preheat the oven to 180°C/Gas 4. Bring the single cream and butter to the boil in a pan and set aside. In a deep, heavy-based pan, mix the glucose and sugar with the water and put over a high heat. Stir well with a spatula and cook until a rich brown colour. Lower the heat, then slowly pour in the cream and butter, stirring well all the time. Finally, add the walnuts and take off the heat.

When the filling is cool, pour into the lined flan ring. Decorate with a lattice of strips cut with the remaining pastry. Bake in the oven for 30 minutes, then leave to cool before removing the ring.

Sweet pastry

Mix the butter, flour and sugar together in a bowl with your fingertips. Gradually add the egg yolks and cream until the dough comes together. Do not overwork. Wrap in clingfilm and chill for at least 2 hours.

189

Pears in Red Wine

6 pears, still a little firm
1 bottle red wine (Pinot or
   Gamay)
200g caster sugar
1 cinnamon stick

1 vanilla pod, split
6 black peppercorns
1 strip of orange peel
4 tablespoons crème de cassis

Serves 6

Peel and core the pears, taking care to leave the stalks in place. Put all the remaining ingredients, except the crème de cassis, into a pan and bring to the boil. Add the pears, make sure they are submerged and cover with greaseproof paper. Simmer for 20 minutes or until tender, then leave to cool. Add the crème de cassis and chill in the refrigerator overnight.

If you want a thicker syrup, decant the liquid and boil until it is reduced by a third. Serve with crème fraîche. If you like, decorate the pears with thin strips of orange peel cooked in sugar syrup.

Roast Figs
with Honey and Pistachios

18 purple figs
90g unsalted butter
ground cinnamon and ginger

200g flower-scented clear honey
juice of 2 lemons
120g peeled pistachios, chopped

Serves 6

Cut the stems off the figs, then cut a cross to about halfway through the fruit. Open up slightly to reveal the speckled red flesh. Put a small knob of butter in each fig and place in a roasting pan. Dust with a little cinnamon and ginger, then drizzle with some of the honey. This can be done in advance.

Preheat the oven to 220°C/Gas 7. Roast the figs in the oven for about 8–10 minutes until the tips have caramelised.

Put three figs on each plate. Place the roasting pan over a medium-high heat on top of the stove and pour in the remaining honey. Cook, stirring all the time, until syrupy. Add the lemon juice and mix well. Pass through a fine sieve and spoon a little over each fig. Sprinkle the chopped pistachios over the figs and serve.

Panna Cotta with Wild Strawberries and Mango Coulis

3 leaves gelatine
2 tablespoons dark rum
600ml single cream
2 vanilla pods, split and seeds
 scraped out
100g caster sugar

peel of 1 orange, no pith
500g wild strawberries

Mango coulis
2 large ripe mangoes
2 tablespoons caster sugar
1 lime juice

Serves 8

Panna cotta literally means cooked cream and is considered Italy's comfort food. This dessert comes from the Piedmont region in Italy and originated in the mid 1800s. It is a delicate dessert and needs a sensitive, seductive wine to accompany it, so try Moscato d'Asti or Vouvray Moelleux.

Soften the gelatine in the rum. In a pan, quickly bring the cream, vanilla pods and seeds, sugar and orange peel to simmering point, stirring to avoid it catching. Immediately take off the heat and stir in the gelatine and rum. Leave to cool, then remove the vanilla pods and orange peel.

Pour the mixture into moulds or ramekins measuring about 5cm across and 4cm high or taller. Put them in the refrigerator and leave to set for at least 8 hours.

To turn out the panna cottas, place them in very hot water for 5–6 seconds. Run a knife around the edge and gently coax out on to a plate. Arrange the wild strawberries and mango coulis decoratively around each panna cotta.

Mango coulis

Peel the mangoes and remove the stones. Place the flesh in a blender with the sugar and lime juice, and blitz until smooth. Pass the mixture through a fine sieve. If the mangoes are not very juicy you may need to add a tablespoon or two of water.

Almond and Orange Cake

50g plain flour
1 teaspoon baking powder
225g caster sugar
250g ground almonds
250g butter, room temperature
1 tablespoon grated zest of
orange

4 free-range eggs
80ml freshly squeezed orange
juice
60g brown sugar
1 tablespoon marmalade
handful of sliced almonds,
toasted

Serves 4

Preheat the oven to 180°C/Gas 4 and butter a 20cm cake tin. Sift the flour, baking powder and caster sugar, and add the ground almonds. Whisk the butter and orange zest together in a bowl until pale, then add the eggs one at a time. Fold in the dry ingredients with a metal spoon, then pour the mixture into the buttered cake tin. Bake in the oven for 45 minutes or until cooked.

Make a syrup by boiling the orange juice and brown sugar together in a pan. Take off the heat and leave to cool.

Once the cake is cooked, prick several times with a skewer to the base and pour on the cooled syrup. Leave the cake to cool completely before brushing on a little warmed marmalade and sprinkling it with a few toasted, sliced almonds. This cake is lovely served with orange segments marinated in a generous splash of whisky and a little demerara sugar.

Vanilla Crème Brûlée with Almond Puff Pastry Sticks

250ml double cream
75ml full-fat milk
1 vanilla pod, scraped
4 egg yolks
3 tablespoons caster sugar, plus
3–4 tablespoons for the topping
2 teaspoons vanilla extract

Almond puff pastry sticks
1 sheet of puff pastry
1 egg, beaten
finely chopped almonds
icing sugar

Serves 4

I like to use large shallow ramekin dishes, for a higher proportion of crunchy brûlée to rich cream. Demerara sugar gives a crunchy, but short-lived topping,

Preheat the oven to 140°C/Gas 1. Put the cream, milk and vanilla pod into a pan and heat to boiling point. Cover and leave to infuse for 10 minutes.

Whisk the egg yolks and 3 tablespoons of sugar together until pale and thick. Add the vanilla extract and pour the boiling cream on to the mixture. Stir well, then pour into four ramekins. Place the ramekins in a bain-marie and cook in the oven for about 20 minutes or until just set. Leave to cool.

Preheat the grill. Sprinkle the cold brûlée with a thin, even layer of sugar, and caramelise under the very hot grill (or use a blowtorch). Repeat several times until you have the desired degree of golden crackling topping. Leave to cool and serve within 2 hours, accompanied by warm almond puff pastry sticks.

Almond puff pastry sticks

Preheat the oven to 190°C/Gas 5. Roll out a sheet of puff pastry to 3mm thickness, brush with beaten egg and sprinkle with finely chopped almonds. Using a long sharp knife, cut strips of pastry 12mm wide and 10cm long. Twist five times and place on a baking sheet. Bake in the oven until golden and crisp, then dust with icing sugar and serve warm with the crème brulée.

Vanilla Flavoured Creamed Rice with Stewed Peaches

225g pudding rice
500–600ml milk
2 vanilla pods, split
80g caster sugar

50ml double cream
200ml condensed milk
50g salted butter
4 ripe peaches

Serves 8

Rinse the rice in cold water and drain. Bring 500ml of the milk to the boil with the vanilla pods and sugar, add the rice and simmer for 30 minutes, stirring occasionally. You may need to add a little more milk to keep it moist. Set aside for 5 minutes. Finish the rice by stirring in the cream, condensed milk and butter.

Plunge the peaches into boiling water for 10 seconds to loosen the skins, then refresh immediately in ice-cold water. This enables you to remove the skins without damaging the flesh or using a peeler. Cut the peaches into six wedges, sprinkle with a little sugar and stew in a saucepan over a medium heat. The amount of sugar depends on taste and how sweet the peaches are; they should not take more than 10 minutes to cook.

To serve, reheat the rice if necessary: it may become a little stodgy, but if this happens just add a drop of warm milk to thin it down. Serve the rice in small deep plates with a big spoonful of the peach compote.

Warm Olive Oil Cake with Lavender and Roasted Figs

2 eggs
80g light brown sugar
80ml olive oil
30ml sweet Madeira
1 heaped teaspoon lavender
  flowers
125g plain flour

½ teaspoon baking powder
10–12 figs, purple variety from
  September crop
80g butter
4 tablespoons clear honey,
  preferably lavender scented
juice of 2 lemons

Serves 6

This is Provence on a plate. Be sure to choose purple figs from September's harvest, when they are at their sweetest and best, and try to find lavender-scented honey. This dessert would be perfect to serve at a dinner party with a late-harvest Riesling wine.

Preheat the oven to 180°C/Gas 4. Butter six little flan moulds, about 5cm x 2cm in size. Whisk the eggs and sugar until frothy. Add the olive oil, Madeira and lavender flowers and continue whisking. Finally fold in the flour and baking powder. Pour the mixture into the buttered moulds and bake in the oven for 12–15 minutes until golden and firm to the touch.

Turn the oven up to 220°C/Gas 7. Cut a cross in each fig from the tip to halfway down. Open the figs up slightly and place a knob of butter in each. Put the figs in a roasting pan, drizzle with honey and bake for 6–8 minutes. Remove the figs and put them on top of the warm cakes.

Put the roasting pan on the stove and pour in the lemon juice. Bring to the boil, stir and spoon the juices over the figs before serving.

Orange and Poppy Seed Shortbreads

1 egg yolk
2 tablespoons crème fraîche
zest of 1 orange
250g plain flour
60g caster sugar
2 tablespoons poppy seeds
60g salted butter, softened
6 oranges

2 tablespoons Cointreau
200ml double cream
100g icing sugar

Orange peel confit
1 orange
3 tablespoons caster sugar

Serves 6

This simple recipe has everything a dessert needs – it's creamy, sweet, sharp and crunchy, and goes very well with a small glass of iced Cointreau. The shortbread keeps well in an airtight container for several days.

Mix the egg yolk, 1 tablespoon of crème fraîche and orange zest together in a bowl. Gently incorporate the flour, sugar, poppy seeds and butter with your fingertips, but do not knead or overwork the dough. Wrap the dough in clingfilm and leave in the refrigerator for 3 hours.

Preheat the oven to 180°C/Gas 4. Roll the dough out on a lightly floured work surface to a thickness of 2–3mm. Cut into 12 equal rectangles and place on a non-stick baking sheet. Bake in the oven for about 15 minutes until light brown and cooked through. Leave to cool completely.

Segment the oranges and douse with Cointreau. Whip the double cream, crème fraîche and icing sugar together until firm. Divide this equally between plates along with the oranges and shortbread biscuits. Decorate with a little orange peel confit.

Orange peel confit

Peel the orange, making sure there is no white pith, and cut into julienne strips. Blanch three times in boiling water. Put in a pan with just enough water to cover and add the sugar. Simmer until tender and translucent. Remove and leave to cool.

Chocolate Mousse with Oranges and Whisky

6 oranges, peeled and
segmented
60ml Drambuie
6 egg whites
325g caster sugar
125ml water
250g butter
6 egg yolks
50g cocoa powder
1 tablespoon chopped
orange peel confit
(page 197)

50ml whisky
125g dark chocolate,
melted
125g milk chocolate,
melted

Genoise
4 eggs
125g caster sugar
25g melted butter
125g flour, sifted
25g cocoa powder

Chocolate glaze
250ml double cream
150g liquid glucose
1 tablespoon vegetable oil
200g dark chocolate,
chopped
1 tablespoon water

Serves 8–10

First the decoration: douse the oranges with Drambuie and chill for 12 hours. Drain the orange for the decoration and soak the genoise in the liquid.

For the mousse, whisk the egg whites until stiff. Dissolve the sugar in the water and boil. Skim and cook until it reaches 120°C. Pour onto the egg whites, whiskng until cool and smooth. Beat the butter, egg yolks and cocoa until light, then mix in the orange peel confit, whisky and chocolate. Fold in meringue and pour on to genoise cake base. Chill for 2 hours. Pour over the glaze and decorate with orange segments.

Genoise

Preheat the oven to 190°C/Gas 5 and butter a 22cm round tin. Whisk the eggs and sugar in a double boiler until stiff, pale and tepid. Take off the heat then fold in the butter, flour and cocoa. Pour the mixture into the buttered tin and bake for 18 minutes. Take out of the tin and cool on a wire rack.

Chocolate glaze

Mix the glaze ingredients together in a pan and bring to the boil. Whisk in the chocolate and bring back to the boil.

Milk Chocolate Mousse Scented with Ginger

150g milk chocolate, roughly
  chopped
250g whipping cream
1 leaf gelatine
40ml white rum, warmed
1 egg
½ teaspoon ground ginger
4 egg whites

110g caster sugar
125g ground hazelnuts
60g flour
75g butter, melted

Ginger confit
7cm piece fresh ginger, peeled
3 tablespoons caster sugar

Serves 6

Milky and chocolatey with a bite of ginger, this is perfect for those who are not keen on dark, bitter chocolate. It keeps for a couple of days in the refrigerator. If you don't have a double boiler, melt the chocolate in a heatproof bowl set over a pan of simmering water.

Melt the chocolate over a double boiler. Whip the cream until stiff. Soak the gelatine in cold water until soft, then melt it in the warm rum. Whisk the gelatine with the egg and ginger in a double boiler until it is pale, frothy and forms peaks. Fold in the chocolate and the cream. Pour into individual ramekins and chill for at least 2 hours.

Make biscuits to decorate the mousse. Preheat the oven to 190°C/Gas 5. Whisk the egg whites with the sugar and ground hazelnuts until smooth. Add the flour and butter, then rest for 1 hour. Spoon heaped teaspoons of the mixture on to a non-stick baking sheet and push down slightly to make circles. Bake for 7–8 minutes until golden brown. Take the biscuits off the tray and, while still hot, curl each one round the handle of a wooden spoon into a cigar shape. Cool. Serve the mousse with biscuits and confit.

Ginger confit

Cut the ginger into thin juliennes. Blanch three times in boiling water. Put in a pan with enough water to cover and add the sugar. Simmer until tender and translucent. Remove and cool.

Chocolate and Pear Tart

300g caster sugar
2 cinnamon sticks
400ml water
3 Williams pears, peeled, cored
  and halved

Sweet pastry
120g butter, softened
250g plain flour

60g caster sugar
1 egg yolk
½ tablespoon double cream

Chocolate filling
120ml double cream
60g butter
250g extra-bitter dark
chocolate, chopped

Serves 6

More chocolate – this time in a tart. Serve cold and on the day it is made, otherwise the pastry will go soft. If you are serving this tart at a dinner party and would like a wine to go with it, then choose a sweet red like Banyuls or even a light Madeira, such as Bual.

Bring the sugar, cinnamon and water to the boil. Add the pears, cover and simmer for 10 minutes or until the pears are tender. Leave to cool in the syrup.

To make the pastry, mix the butter, flour and sugar together in a bowl with your fingertips. Gradually add the egg yolk and cream until the dough comes together. Do not overwork. Wrap in clingfilm and chill for at least 2 hours.

Preheat the oven to 180°C/Gas 4 and butter a 22cm fluted tart tin. Roll out the dough on a lightly floured surface and line the buttered tart tin. Cut the edges flush with the sides and prick the base with a fork. Line with greaseproof paper and dry beans and bake in the oven for 15 minutes. Remove the paper and beans and put back in the oven for 10 minutes until golden and fully cooked. Leave to cool in the tin.

Chocolate filling

Bring the cream to the boil in a pan. Add the butter, cut into small pieces, and chocolate and whisk well until compeletely melted.

Pour the chocolate filling into the tart. Drain the pears on a tea towel until completely dry. Slice them across, fan out and place in the tart, keeping their shape. Chill for 45 minutes before taking out of the tin and slicing.

Chocolate Chip Cookies with Brandy Soaked Prunes

260g caster sugar
200ml water
24 Agen prunes, pitted
200ml brandy
110g butter
80g soft dark brown sugar
1 egg

1 teaspoon vanilla extract
250g plain flour, sifted
½ teaspoon salt
½ teaspoon baking powder
80g extra-bitter dark chocolate,
  chopped into chips
300ml crème fraîche, to serve

Serves 6

This is indulgent and calorie-laden – but tell yourself that prunes are good for you. Try to find Agen prunes, which are from south-western France, as they are soft, juicy and sweet. You need to start this recipe by marinating the prunes a week ahead.

For the prunes, mix 180g of caster sugar with the water in a pan and bring to the boil for 3–4 minutes. Take the pan off the heat and leave to cool. When tepid, add the prunes and brandy. Cover tightly and leave in the refrigerator for at least a week – these prunes can keep for years but seldom get the chance!

Preheat the oven to 190°C/Gas 5. Cream the butter with brown sugar and remaining caster sugar, egg and vanilla extract. Gradually work in the flour, salt and baking powder, then quickly mix in the chocolate. Spoon on to a non-stick baking sheet and shape into rounds. The mix should make around 6 cookies. Bake in the oven for 10 minutes and leave to cool on a wire rack.

To serve, drain the prunes and reduce the marinade in a pan over a high heat until syrupy. Put the prunes back in the pan with the reduced marinade, cover and reheat. Place three cookies on each plate with prunes in between and a generous spoonful of crème fraîche.

Bitter Chocolate Cake and Kirsch-soaked Cherries

75g plain flour
75g cocoa powder
75g ground hazelnuts
9 egg yolks
150g caster sugar
6 egg whites
1 tablespoon butter, melted
250g jar of Griottines

chocolate curls and icing sugar
Mousse filling
400g butter
220g extra-bitter dark
chocolate, broken into pieces
40g cocoa powder
6 eggs, separated
280g sugar

Serves 10

This is almost a forêt noire, but in my view better and lighter. It's more of a cake to serve in the afternoon than a dessert, although it would be a good choice if you were only serving two courses. Try to find Griottines, which are morello cherries soaked in Kirsch syrup.

Preheat the oven to 200°C/Gas 6 and butter and line a 20cm cake tin. Sift the flour, cocoa and ground hazelnuts. Whisk the egg yolks and sugar until pale and stiff and fold into dry ingredients. Whisk the egg whites until stiff and fold in with the melted butter. Pour into the cake tin and bake in the oven for 18–20 minutes. Leave to cool in the tin. When cold, cut across in half and trim the top to make a flat surface.

Drain the cherries and moisten both halves of the chocolate sponge with the Kirsch syrup. Spread some of the mousse over the first layer of sponge, add the cherries in an even layer and then more mousse. Place the second layer of cake on top, moisten with a little more Kirsch syrup, then cover completely with chocolate mousse. Chill for at least 4 hours before cutting. Decorate with chocolate curls and dust with icing sugar.

Mousse filling

Gently melt the butter and chocolate in a double boiler. Do not allow to overheat. Take off the heat and mix in the cocoa and egg yolks. Whisk the egg whites; once they are frothy, add the sugar and continue to whisk until stiff. Fold this into the chocolate.

Stocks and Sauces

White Chicken Stock

2kg chicken bones or wing tips
1 calf's foot, split
5 litres water
1 onion

1 small leek
2 celery sticks
2 sprigs of thyme
6 parsley stalks

Makes about 4 litres

Place the bones and calf's foot in a large pan, cover with the water and bring to the boil. Skim off the scum and fat that comes to the surface. Turn the heat down, add the remaining ingredients and simmer for 1½ hours, skimming occasionally. Pass through a fine sieve and leave to cool. This can be kept in the refrigerator for up to 5 days, or frozen.

Veal Stock

1.5kg veal knuckle bones, chopped
1 calf's foot, split
1 large onion, roughly chopped
2 large carrots, roughly chopped
1 celery stick, roughly chopped

5 litres water
2 garlic cloves
2 sprigs thyme
½ tablespoon tomato purée

Makes about 3.5 litres

Preheat the oven to 220°C/Gas 7. Put the bones and calf's foot in a roasting pan and roast in the oven, turning occasionally until brown all over. Transfer to a large pan.

Put the onion, carrots and celery into the roasting pan and roast until golden. Pour off any excess fat and put the vegetables into the pan with the bones. Put the roasting pan over a high heat. Add 500ml water to deglaze the pan. Scrape the bottom to loosen the caramelised sugars, then pour into the pan with the bones.

Add the remaining ingredients and remaining water and bring to the boil. Skim off the scum and fat. Turn down the heat and simmer gently for 3½ hours, skimming occasionally. Pass through a fine sieve and leave to cool.

Beef Stock for Soup

3kg beef bones, chopped
3 pig's trotters, split
2 onions, roughly chopped
1 carrot, roughly chopped
2 celery sticks, roughly chopped
2 bay leaves

1 sprig thyme
1 bunch parsley stalks
2 teaspoons peppercorns
3 beefsteak tomatoes, chopped
1 leek top (green part)

Makes about 5 litres

Preheat the oven to 220°C/Gas 7. Put the bones and trotters in a roasting pan and roast in the oven, turning occasionally, until brown all over. Transfer to a large pan and pour in enough water to cover by 15cm.

Pour off some of the fat from the roasting pan, add the onions, carrot and celery, and roast until golden. Add the vegetables and all the other ingredients to the bones. Put the roasting pan over a high heat. Add 500ml water to deglaze the pan. Scrape the bottom to loosen the caramelised sugars, then pour into the pan with the bones. Bring to the boil, skim off the scum, then lower the heat and simmer for 2½ hours, skimming frequently. Strain and chill. Store in the refrigerator for a week, or freeze.

Court Bouillon

2 carrots, peeled
white part 1 leek
1 celery stick
½ fennel bulb
4 shallots, peeled
2 small white onions, peeled
1.5 litres water

1 bottle dry white wine
2 tablespoons white wine
 vinegar
1 bouquet garni
25g coarse sea salt
1 tablespoon cracked black or
 white peppercorns

Makes about 3½ litres

Slice the vegetables into thin 3mm rounds. Bring the water, wine and vinegar to the boil, add all the vegetables, bouquet garni, salt and the peppercorns tied in a little muslin bag. Simmer for 15 minutes until the vegetables are cooked but still a little crunchy. Strain and chill. This can be kept in the refrigerator for 3–4 days.

Fish Stock

1kg bones and heads from white
fish (sole, whiting, turbot)
4 tablespoons butter
1 small onion, peeled and
roughly chopped

1 celery stick, roughly chopped
60g dry white wine
2 litres water
6 parsley stalks
1 bay leaf

Makes about 2 litres

Remove any gills from the fish heads, then soak the heads and bones in cold water for 3–4 hours. Roughly chop the fish bones and heads. Melt the butter in a deep pan and sweat the onion and celery over a low heat until softened. Add the fish bones and heads and cook for 2–3 minutes, stirring frequently.

Pour in the wine, turn up the heat and reduce by half. Add the water and herbs and bring to the boil, skimming frequently. Lower the heat and simmer, uncovered, for 25 minutes.

Strain through a muslin-lined sieve and leave to cool.

Chicken Jus

1kg chicken bones, chopped small
3 shallots, chopped
100ml dry white wine
2.5 litres chicken stock (page 206)

Makes about 2 litres

Preheat the oven to 220°C/Gas 7. Put the bones in a roasting pan and roast in the oven, turning occasionally, until brown all over. Transfer to a deep pan.

Brown the shallots in the roasting pan, stirring frequently. Add the wine and stir to loosen all the residue. Boil to reduce by half, then pour into the pan with the bones. Add the stock and bring to the boil. Simmer for 45 minutes, skimming occasionally, then strain.

Red Wine Sauce

120g beef trimmings (bone or
  sinew), optional
a little olive oil
1 bottle full-bodied red wine
  (Syrah or Shiraz)
100ml port

1 onion, peeled and sliced
2 shallots, peeled and sliced
3 strips smoked bacon, chopped
1 teaspoon cracked white and
  black peppercorns
2 litres veal stock

Makes 1.5 litres

If you have some beef trimmings, fry them in a pan with a little olive oil until crisp.
Drain off the fat, add the wine and port and reduce by half.

Heat a little olive oil in another pan and cook the onion, shallots and bacon until
well browned. Add the peppercorns and then pour in the reduced wine, followed by
the stock. Bring to the boil and skim. Turn down the heat and simmer for 35 minutes.
Pass through a fine sieve. To serve with steaks, bring the sauce to the boil and
reduce until slightly thickened. Take off the heat and whisk in a little butter, cut into
small pieces.

Tarragon Sauce

2 shallots, peeled and finely
  chopped
2 tablespoons unsalted butter
2 tablespoons tarragon vinegar
100ml dry white wine

400ml chicken stock
100ml double cream
salt and white pepper
5 tablespoons tarragon leaves
  chopped

Makes 250ml

Sweat the shallots in half the butter over a low heat until softened but not coloured.
Deglaze the pan with the vinegar and wine, then reduce until nearly dry. Pour in the
stock and reduce until syrupy. Add the cream and boil for 2 minutes, then whisk in
the remaining butter, season to taste and add the tarragon just before serving with
chicken or poached fish.

Hollandaise Sauce

225g unsalted butter
2 teaspoons white wine vinegar
1 teaspoon cracked white peppercorns

pinch of salt
2 tablespoons water
4 egg yolks
lemon juice, to taste

Makes 150ml

Melt the butter in a small pan over low heat until it foams. Spoon off the foam and let the butter settle. Remove the clarified butter with a ladle, discarding the whitish residue in the base of the pan.

Boil the vinegar with the pepper and salt, then take off the heat. Add the water and egg yolks, transfer to a double boiler (not too hot) and whisk for about 8–10 minutes until the egg yolks are light and creamy. Do not let the mixture get too hot. Take off the heat and, whisking continuously, pour in the clarified butter. Pass through a fine sieve, and add a little lemon juice to taste.

Aïoli

5 garlic cloves, peeled
2 egg yolks
1 teaspoon Dijon mustard

2 teaspoons white wine vinegar
salt and cayenne pepper
275ml light olive oil

Makes 275ml

Slice the garlic lengthways, removing any green shoots, then put the garlic in a blender with the egg yolks, mustard, vinegar, salt and cayenne pepper, and blend at full speed. Gradually trickle in the olive oil while the blender is running. After half of the oil has been incorporated, stop and scrape down the sides of the blender with a spatula. Continue to trickle in the oil, scraping the sides of the blender once or twice more, and adding 1–2 tablespoons cold water with the last of the oil to thin the consistency slightly, until you have a smooth garlic mayonnaise.

Herb Vinaigrette

2 egg yolks
1 teaspoon Dijon mustard
1½ tablespoons tarragon vinegar
salt and white pepper
150ml extra virgin olive oil

300ml vegetable oil
1 tablespoon each of chives, flat
leaf parsley and tarragon,
chopped

Makes 500ml

Put the egg yolks in a blender with the mustard, vinegar, salt and pepper, and blend at high speed, slowly adding the olive and vegetable oils, a little at a time. After a third of the oil has been incorporated, add the herbs. Continue to blend, adding the oils a little at a time. The vinaigrette should have the consistency of pouring cream. If the mixture becomes too thick, add a few drops of cold water to the blender. If you want to remove the herbs, pass the vinaigrette through a fine sieve. Chill for up to 2 weeks.

Tomato Vinaigrette

Makes 500ml

Replace the herbs with 1 heaped teaspoon tomato purée and 1 heaped tablespoon of tomato 'fondu': 4 ripe tomatoes, peeled, deseeded and chopped, then cooked gently in a little olive oil until the mixture is thick and dry. Instead of the pepper in the herb vinaigrette, use a few drops of Tabasco sauce.

Béarnaise Sauce

250g unsalted butter
2 shallots, peeled and finely
  chopped
3 tablespoons snipped tarragon
3 tablespoons white wine
vinegar or tarragon vinegar

1 teaspoon crushed white
  peppercorns
1 tablespoon water
4 egg yolks
salt and pepper
2 tablespoons snipped chervil

Makes 175ml

Melt the butter in a small pan over a low heat until it foams. Spoon off the foam and let the butter settle. Remove the clarified butter with a ladle, discarding the whitish residue in the base of the pan.

Put the shallots in a pan with the tarragon, vinegar, pepper and the water and boil to reduce by half. Cool. When cold, add the egg yolks and whisk in a double boiler for 8–10 minutes until the yolks are light and creamy. Take off the heat and, whisking continuously, pour in the clarified butter. Season and add the chervil before serving.

Sauce Paloise

Makes 175ml

Use fresh mint instead of tarragon and chervil. Delicious with grilled lamb.

Sauce Choron

Makes 175ml

Peel, deseed and chop 5 ripe plum tomatoes and sweat in a little butter to remove excess moisture. Add to the finished Béarnaise sauce.

Pesto

200g basil leaves	pinch of salt
20g pine nuts	50g Parmesan cheese, grated
3 walnuts, roughly chopped	150–200ml extra virgin olive oil

Makes 250ml

This intensely basil-flavoured pesto can be made in a mortar and pestle, and if you are making just a small amount and have plenty of time to spare, go for it. Otherwise, double or treble the quantities given here and make a big batch in a blender; no one will be the wiser.

Put the basil, nuts and salt in a large mortar and grind with a pestle to form a coarse paste. Work the Parmesan into the paste, then gradually beat in the olive oil with a wooden spoon until you have a thick sauce.

Alternatively, place all ingredients (begin with the smaller amount of oil) except the cheese in a blender and purée briefly at high speed. Add the cheese and blend for a few seconds. The secret of making pesto in a blender is not to overmix it. If the basil is blended for too long it will become hot and lose its bright green colour.

If you want the pesto for pasta, grilled fish or to garnish soup, then keep it fairly coarse and dry. If it is for mixing into a sauce or to use as salad dressing with a little balsamic vinegar, use more oil and blend until smooth.

If stored in a clean airtight jar with a film of oil on top of the pesto, it can be kept in the refrigerator for up to 2 weeks.

Conversions

Liquid equivalents

METRIC	IMPERIAL	AMERICAN
15ml	1 tablespoon	
60ml	2fl oz	¼ cup
90ml	3fl oz	
100ml	3 ½ fl oz	
125ml	4fl oz	¼ cup
150ml	5fl oz	⅔ cup
180ml	6fl oz	¾ cup
200ml	7fl oz	
250ml	8fl oz	1 cup
300ml	10fl oz (½ pint)	1¼ cups
375ml	12fl oz	1¼ cups
500ml	15fl oz (I pint)	2 cups
600ml	1pint	2½ cups
1 litre	1I pints	4 cups (1 quart)

Weight equivalents

METRIC	IMPERIAL	METRIC	IMPERIAL
15g	½oz	300g	10oz
20g	¾oz	325g	11oz
30g	1oz	350g	12oz
60g	2oz	375g	13oz
90g	3oz	400g	14oz
100g	3½oz	425g	15oz
120g	4oz	450g	1 lb
150g	5oz	500g	1 lb 2oz
175g	6oz	750g	1½lb
200g	7oz	900g	2lb
225g	8oz	1kg	2¼lb
250g	9oz	1.4kg	3lb

Oven temperatures

	°C	°F	gas
very cool	100–120	225–250	G–½
	140	275	1
cool	150	300	2
warm	160	325	3
moderate	180	350	4
moderately hot	190	375	5
	200	400	6
hot	220	425	7
very hot	230	450	8
	240–250	475–500	9–10

Notes:
1 teaspoon = 5ml
1 tablespoon = 15ml
spoon measurements are level
unless otherwise stated

pepper: use freshly ground black pepper unless otherwise stated

fresh ginger juice: grate a large piece (50–100g) of fresh ginger root into a small bowl, add 1–2 teaspoons dry white wine and leave for 1 hour. Pour the grated ginger and wine through a sieve into another bowl, pressing the ginger to extract all the flavour.

braising: all braised meat and poultry dishes improve with keeping, so make them the day before you want to serve them and leave to chill in their liquid; reheat just before serving.

turbot: I generally try to use large turbot of 8lb or more: the flesh will be firm, meaty and moist, and fish of this size is almost certainly wild, which is far superior to farmed fish.

lobsters: a whole lobster can be killed by plunging it into boiling water for 10–15 seconds. However, some recipes call for freshly killed lobster, and you should do this just before you begin the recipe. Make sure that the claws are secured with rubber bands, then place the lobster on a chopping board and hold its tail firmly, protecting your hand with a tea towel. Using a strong, very sharp, pointed knife, quickly and firmly pierce the lobster between the eyes – this kills it instantly.

Index

First published in Great Britain in 2010 by Weidenfeld & Nicolson

1 3 5 7 9 10 8 6 4 2

Text copyright © Michel Roux Jr 2010
Design and layout copyright © Weidenfeld & Nicolson 2010

Edited by Kathy Steer, Nicola Crossley & Cherry Ekins. Designed by Julyan Bayes
Photography by Cristian Barnett, Tara Fisher and Jean Cazals

A CIP catalogue record for this book is available from the British Library.
ISBN-978 0 297 86309 0

The Orion Publishing Group's policy is to use papers that are natural, renewable and recyclable products and made from wood grown in sustainable forests. The logging and manufacturing processes are expected to conform to the environmental regulations of the country of origin.

Printed in Italy

Weidenfeld & Nicolson

The Orion Publishing Group Ltd
Orion House
5 Upper St Martin's Lane
London WC2H 9EA

An Hachette UK Company

www.orionbooks.co.uk

FSC
Mixed Sources
Product group from well-managed forests and other controlled sources
Cert no. CQ-COC-000012
www.fsc.org
© 1996 Forest Stewardship Council